Report on

THE ENIAC

(Electronic Numerical Integrator and Computer)

Developed under the supervision of the
Ordnance Department, United States Army

OPERATING MANUAL

UNIVERSITY OF PENNSYLVANIA

Moore School of Electrical Engineering

PHILADELPHIA, PENNSYLVANIA

June 1, 1946

A REPORT ON THE ENIAC

(Electronic Numerical Integrator and Computer)

Report of Work under Contract No. W-670-ORD-4926

Between

Ordnance Department, United States Army
Washington, D. C.

and

The University of Pennsylvania
Moore School of Electrical Engineering
Philadelphia, Pa.

ENIAC OPERATING MANUAL

by

Dr. Arthur W. Burks

and

Dr. Harry D. Huskey

Moore School of Electrical Engineering
University of Pennsylvania

INTRODUCTION TO REPORT ON THE

ELECTRONIC NUMERICAL INTEGRATOR AND COMPUTOR (ENIAC)

0. INTRODUCTION

The Report on the ENIAC consists of five separately bound parts, as
follows:

1) ENIAC Operating Manual

2) ENIAC Maintenance Manual

3) Part I, Technical Description of the ENIAC

   Volume I – Chapters I to VI

4) Part I, Technical Description of the ENIAC

   Volume II – Chapters VII to XI

5) Part II, Technical Description of the ENIAC

Included with the Operating Manual and Parts I and II of the Technical Descriptic
are all drawings (see Table 0.3 below) which are required for understanding these
reports. The Maintenance Manual assumes access to the complete file of ENIAC
drawings.

Part I of the Technical Description is intended for those who wish
to have a general understanding of how the ENIAC works, without concerning them-
selves with the details of the circuits; it assumes no knowledge of electronics
or circuit theory. Part II is intended for those who require a detailed understanding of the circuits. Its organization, to a great extent, duplicates that
of Part I so as to make cross referencing between the two parts easy.

The ENIAC Operating Manual contains a complete set of instructions
for operating the ENIAC. It includes very little explanatory material, and
hence assumes familiarity with Part I of the Technical Description of the ENIAC.
The ENIAC Maintenance Manual includes description of the various test units and
procedures for testing, as well as a list of common and probable sources of
trouble. It assumes a complete understanding of the circuits of the ENIAC, i.e.,
a knowledge of both Parts I and II of the Technical Description of the ENIAC.

The Report on the ENIAC and the complete file of ENIAC drawings constitute a complete description and set of instructions for operation and maintenance of the machine. The drawings carry a number of the form PX-n-m. The following tables give the classification according to this numbering system.

TABLE 0.1	
Values of n	Division
1	General
2	Test Equipment
3	Racks and Panels
4	Trays, Cables, Adaptors, and Load Boxes
5	Accumulators
6	High Speed Multiplier
7	Function Table
8	Master Programmer
9	Cycling Unit and Initiating Unit
10	Divider and Square Rooter
11	Constant Transmitter
12	Printer
13	Power Supplies

TABLE 0.2	
Values of n	Subject
101-200	Wiring Diagrams
201-300	Mechanical Drawings
301-400	Report Drawings
401-500	Illustration Problem Set-Ups.

The reader of this report will be primarily interested in the types of drawings listed in the following paragraphs. A table on page 4 gives the corresponding drawing number for each unit of the ENIAC.

1) Front Panel Drawings. These drawings show in some detail the switches, sockets, etc., for each panel of each unit. They contain the essential instructions for setting up a problem on the ENIAC.

2) Front View Drawings. There is one of these drawings for each kind of panel used in the various units of the ENIAC. These show the relative position of the trays and the location of the various neon lights. Since these drawings show the neon lights, they can be used to check the proper operation of the various units.

3) Block Diagrams. These drawings illustrate the logical essentials of the internal circuits of each unit. That is, resistors, condensers, and some other electrical details are not shown; but complete channels (paths of pulses or gates representing numbers or program signals) are shown in all their multiplicity. These drawings will be of interest to those who are interested in Parts I and II of the Technical Report.

4) Cross-section Diagrams. These drawings are electronically complet except that only one channel is shown where there is more than one. Thus, these drawings show every resistor and condenser and any other electronic elements belonging to any circuit. These drawings will be of particular interest to the maintenance personnel and to those reading Part II of the technical report.

5) Detail Drawings. All other drawings of the ENIAC come under this heading. A complete file of drawings is available at the location of the ENIAC.

Table 0.3
ENIAC DRAWINGS

Unit	Front Panel	Front View	Block Diagram	Cross - Section
Initiating Unit	PX-9-302 9-302R	PX-9-305	PX-9-307	
Cycling Unit	PX-9-303 9-303R	PX-9-304	PX-9-307	
Accumulator	PX-5-301	PX-5-305	PX-5-304	PX-5-115
Multiplier	PX-6-302 6-302R 6-303 6-303R 6-304 6-304R	PX-6-309	PX-6-308	PX-6-112A 6-112B
Function Table	PX-7-302 7-302R 7-303 7-303R	PX-7-305	PX-7-304	PX-7-117 7-118
Divider and Square Rooter	PX-10-301 10-301R	PX-10-302	PX-10-304	
Constant Transmitter	PX-11-302 11-302R 11-303 11-303R 11-304 11-304R	PX-11-306	PX-11-307	PX-11-116 11-309 (C.T. and R.
Printer	PX-12-301 12-301R 12-302 12-302R 12-303 12-303R	PX-12-306	PX-12-307	PX-12-115
Master Programmer	PX-8-301 8-301R 8-302 8-302R	PX-8-303	PX-8-304	PX-8-102

Other drawings of particular interest:

Floor Plan	PX-1-302	IBM Punch and	PX-12-112
A.C. Wiring	PX-1-303	Plugboard	PX-12-305
IBM Reader and	PX-11-119	Pulse Amplifier and	PX-4-302
plugboard	PX-11-305	Block Diagram	PX-4-301

Interconnection of Multiplier and Accumulators PX-6-311
Interconnection of Divider and Accumulators PX-10-307

The front view drawings and the large front panel drawings (whose numbers do not end with "R") are bound as a part of the Operator's Manual.

Included with the report is a folder containing all the drawings listed in the above table except the large front panel (see above) drawings.

1. GENERAL INSTRUCTIONS FOR OPERATING PERSONNEL

1. Inform maintenance personnel immediately of any trouble and note same in the log book.

2. Occasionally check the filament fuse indicator lights (refer to front view drawings bound in this volume); if any are out turn off the d-c power (switch is located on a-c distribution panel, see PX-1-304).

3. If ENIAC shuts down from overheating do not try to restart; call maintenance personnel. If any panel runs consistently much hotter than the others, do the same.

4. The d-c power should be turned on only with operation switch (either on cycling unit or on the hand control) turned to "continuous". After the d-c has been on a few seconds it may be turned to either of the other two positions. Failure to follow this rule causes certain d-c fuses to blow, -240 and -415 in particular.

5. As a general matter certain units not being used may have their heaters turned off. In such cases it is unnecessary to remove the d-c power or even to turn off the d-c power when turning on these units. On the other hand the three panels of the constant transmitter must be turned on or off simultaneously.

6. Do not remove any covers, front or back.

7. Do not open d-c fuse cabinet with the d-c power turned on. This not only exposes a person to voltage differences of around 1500 volts but the

person may be burned by flying pieces of molten fuse wire in case a fuse should blow.

8. Padlocks are provided for locking the d-c power off.   Lock the power off and carry the key with you as long as you are working on the machine.

9. Do not remove accumulator interconnector plugs, or function table or IBM machine connector cables, while the d-c is on. All other front panel plugs may be safely moved while the power is on.

10. Do not pull directly on wire or cable; always use the plug case as a grip.

11. Do not put sharp bends in cables or hang anything on them.

12. Do not leave cables dangling on the floor.

13. Do not pound or force plugs; if they do not respond to steady pressure notify maintenance personnel.

14. Do not leave IBM cable connectors or portable function table connectors lying out in the open, keep in the receptacles provided. Also, make use of the ramps to protect the cables of any such units which are connected to the ENIAC.

15. Do not force any switches.

16. Keep the door to the room closed to keep out dust, avoid stirring up or producing dust.

17. Always move the portable function tables with care. Keep the brakes on when not moving them.

2. PROBLEM SET UP REMARKS

2.1. NEED FOR SYSTEMATIC CHECKS

Since the ENIAC makes use of a hierarchy of channels (first, in that a

number of units may be carrying on computations simultaneously; second, in that
it always handles ten to twenty digits of a number simultaneously; and third,
in that certain units use a coded system giving four channels for each digit)
running a standard check problem is not a sufficient check on the accuracy of
the results. Thus, in arranging a problem for the ENIAC provision should be
made for occasional systematic checks of all the units.

Procedures for systematic checking are described in some detail in
the maintenance manual. Brief procedures will be outlined here for the numerical
units. The following test procedures are not comprehensive tests and the ex-
perienced operator will perhaps use variations of them. In particular, the
tests given below are not designed to check the operation of the various program
controls. However, they are designed to check the numerical circuits in each
unit and to a considerable extent check the program control used to carry out
the test.

2.2. TESTING AN ACCUMULATOR

Cards should be prepared as follows:

1. P 11111 11111

2. P 00000 00001

The numbers should be so placed on a card that one group in the constant transmitter, say A_{LR}, corresponds to these numbers. Next, a master programmer stepper
should be used to transmit the first number into the accumulators which are to
be tested eighteen times. At this time the accumulators should read

M 99999 99998

and all stages of each decade have been checked as well as the delayed carry-over
circuits. Now the stepper (used above) should cause the reader to read the next
card and the number to be transmitted to the accumulators twice. This should

give

P 00000 00000

and checks the direct carry-over circuits. Note that this test assumes that
the significant figure switch is set to "10". If this is not so the operator
can modify the above procedure to take care of this.

This test does not check the following circuits (for a complete checking procedure see the maintenance manual):

Transmission circuits   Input channels (except for the one used)
Clearing circuits   Program controls (except for the one used)
Repeater ring

2.3. TESTING THE MULTIPLIER

The following set of cards should be prepared.

Card	Multiplier A_{LR} (say)	Multiplicand B_{LR} (say)
1	P 00000 00000	P 11111 11111
2	P 11111 11111	P 11111 11111
3	P 11111 11111	P 22222 22222
. . . .	. . . .	. . . .
10	P 11111 11111	P 99999 99999
11	P 22222 22222	P 11111 11111
12	P 22222 22222	P 22222 22222
. . . .	. . . .	. . . .
82	P 99999 99999	P 99999 99999
83	P 11111 11111	M 11111 11111
84	M 11111 11111	P 11111 11111
85	M 11111 11111	M 11111 11111

On a second set of cards, or on these same cards in different fields the proper answers should be punched. Note that these answers will depend upon when ten or twenty digit products are used, that is, whether the product accumulators are used as ten or twenty digit accumulators.

There are two methods of using these cards to check the numerical circuits of the multiplier. One is to have the answer on the same card and arrange for its transmission to the product accumulators with its sign changed (or the sign of one of the factors may be changed). In this case the whole sequence of cards in run and the presence of "zero" in the product accumulators indicates (with high probability since there could be compensating errors) that the numerical circuits are all right.

A second method is to run the test and cause the answers to be punched on other cards. These results may then be compared with standard answers by use of the reproducing punch.

This procedure does not check the following:

Rounding off circuits

Program controls. (other than the one used).

2.4. TO TEST A FUNCTION TABLE

An accumulator is used to build up the argument. A program control on the function table has its function switch set to "-2" and a second switch has its argument set to "+2".

The programming is so arranged that the "-2" program is activated and the output sent to an accumulator associated with the printer. The result is punched on a card, "one" is added to the argument, and the process repeated.

The master programmer can be used to repeat the "-2" program 96 times and then alternately activate the "-2" and the "+2" program four more times. (Or various other schemes may be devised to obtain all 104 entries to the function table.) The cards punched in this manner can then be compared with a standard deck.

Note that the above check is <u>not</u> a systematic check of the numerical circuits as a whole. In other words this check should be repeated if any switches on the portable table (or on panel No. 2) are changed.

Furthermore, the above procedure does not check the various program controls of the function table.

2.5. TO TEST THE DIVIDER AND SQUARE ROOTER

The divider and square rooter can best be checked by performing test division problems and square root problems. Drawing PX-10-111 gives the neons which should be lit at various places in the process. The operator can check against this by going through the problem at one addition time.

2.6. CONSTANT TRANSMITTER TEST PROCEDURE

The 1, 2, 2', 4 channels in the constant transmitter can all be checked simultaneously by reading cards with nine punches on them. Since it is undesirable that the same number be punched in all columns of a card (this weakens a card increasing the probability of "jamming" in the feeding mechanism of the IBM machines) it is suggested that cards be prepared as follows.

1) 9's in groups A_{LR} and B_{LR}

2) 9's in groups C_{LR} and D_{LR}

3) 9's in groups E_{LR} and F_{LR}

4) 9's in groups G_{LR} and H_{LR}

5) Four more cards similar to above but with minus punches.

The programming should be arranged so that the numbers are transmitted into accumulators when they can be inspected visually or perhaps punched on other cards and compared with a standard deck using the reproducing punch.

Note that J_{LR} and K_{LR} should be checked in a similar manner. (These only need be checked for the numbers used in the set-up provided they are re-checked any time that some of the switch settings are changed.)

This procedure does not check all the program controls.

2.7. PRINTER TEST PROCEDURE

The printer can be tested by causing all possible digits in each channel to be punched and by checking the PM delays. The following cards should be prepared.

1) P 01234 56789

2) P 11111 11101

3) P 11111 11011

. . . .

10) P 01111 11111

11) P 11111 11111

The programming should be arranged to cause the numbers on the test cards to be read by the IBM reader, transmitted to the printing accumulators, and the result punched. The resulting cards may be compared with a standard deck by use of the reproducing punch.

Card number one has the numbers 0 to 9 punched in it to prevent the same digit from being punched all across a card.

If any decades of the master programmer are used in printing they may be checked at this time by transmitting the program pulse (used to activate the above sequence) into each decade direct input.

This constitutes a complete test of the printer.

2.8. TESTING FOR TRANSIENT FAILURES

If transient failures are suspected a master programmer stepper should be used to repeat the appropriate test (such as one of those above) a large number of times.

In case of an accumulator this can be done using only one card (say, P 99999 99999) and using a second program control set to αC (receive on α and correct) to obtain the one pulse in the units decade.

For the multiplier it becomes necessary to punch the answers on the cards with the factors (see 2.3) and cause these to be transmitted to the product accumulators for each multiplication. If more than ten digit answers are used the adjusted answer to card 83 must be carefully prepared in order to get minus the answer from the constant transmitter to the product accumulators (since the constant transmitter only complements at most ten digits at a time).

Repetition of a function table test is straight forward. It may be worth while to receive into a twenty digit accumulator and repeat the transmission 10^4 times, say, and see if the proper number is obtained.

The square root of zero is perhaps the easiest test to repeat on the divider-square rooter.

The constant transmitter can be caused to transmit any group repeatedly to some accumulator. Dust particles may cause transient relay failures, so avoid stirring up dust in the ENIAC room. Also, if any relay case is removed, always replace in exactly the same position in order not to disturb dust inside the case.

Transient failures in the printer are probably relay failures. See maintenance manual for list of probable failures.

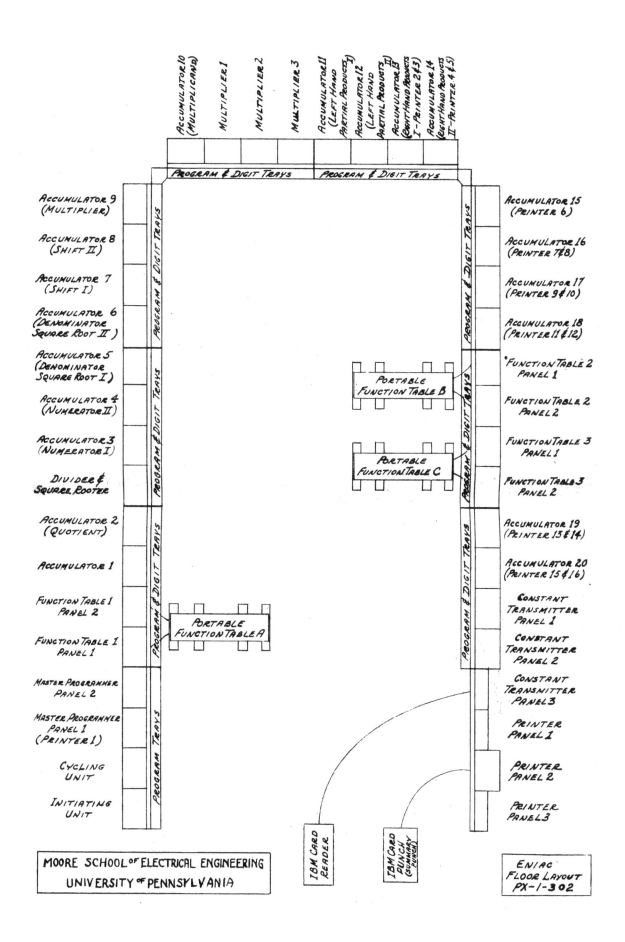

ACCUMULATOR 10 (MULTIPLICAND)
MULTIPLIER 1
MULTIPLIER 2
MULTIPLIER 3
ACCUMULATOR 11 (LEFT HAND PARTIAL PRODUCTS I)
ACCUMULATOR 12 (LEFT HAND PARTIAL PRODUCTS II)
ACCUMULATOR 13 (RIGHT HAND PRODUCTS I - PRINTER 2 & 3)
ACCUMULATOR 14 (RIGHT HAND PRODUCTS II - PRINTER 4 & 5)

PROGRAM & DIGIT TRAYS   PROGRAM & DIGIT TRAYS

ACCUMULATOR 9 (MULTIPLIER)
ACCUMULATOR 8 (SHIFT II)
ACCUMULATOR 7 (SHIFT I)
ACCUMULATOR 6 (DENOMINATOR SQUARE ROOT II)
ACCUMULATOR 5 (DENOMINATOR SQUARE ROOT I)
ACCUMULATOR 4 (NUMERATOR II)
ACCUMULATOR 3 (NUMERATOR I)
DIVIDER & SQUARE ROOTER
ACCUMULATOR 2 (QUOTIENT)
ACCUMULATOR 1
FUNCTION TABLE 1 PANEL 2
FUNCTION TABLE 1 PANEL 1
MASTER PROGRAMMER PANEL 2
MASTER PROGRAMMER PANEL 1 (PRINTER 1)
CYCLING UNIT
INITIATING UNIT

PROGRAM & DIGIT TRAYS
PROGRAM & DIGIT TRAYS
PROGRAM & DIGIT TRAYS
PROGRAM & DIGIT TRAYS
PROGRAM TRAYS

PORTABLE FUNCTION TABLE A

PORTABLE FUNCTION TABLE B

PORTABLE FUNCTION TABLE C

PROGRAM & DIGIT TRAYS
PROGRAM & DIGIT TRAYS
PROGRAM & DIGIT TRAYS

ACCUMULATOR 15 (PRINTER 6)
ACCUMULATOR 16 (PRINTER 7 & 8)
ACCUMULATOR 17 (PRINTER 9 & 10)
ACCUMULATOR 18 (PRINTER 11 & 12)
FUNCTION TABLE 2 PANEL 1
FUNCTION TABLE 2 PANEL 2
FUNCTION TABLE 3 PANEL 1
FUNCTION TABLE 3 PANEL 2
ACCUMULATOR 19 (PRINTER 13 & 14)
ACCUMULATOR 20 (PRINTER 15 & 16)
CONSTANT TRANSMITTER PANEL 1
CONSTANT TRANSMITTER PANEL 2
CONSTANT TRANSMITTER PANEL 3
PRINTER PANEL 1
PRINTER PANEL 2
PRINTER PANEL 3

IBM CARD READER

IBM CARD PUNCH (SUMMARY PUNCH)

MOORE SCHOOL OF ELECTRICAL ENGINEERING
UNIVERSITY OF PENNSYLVANIA

ENIAC FLOOR LAYOUT PX-1-302

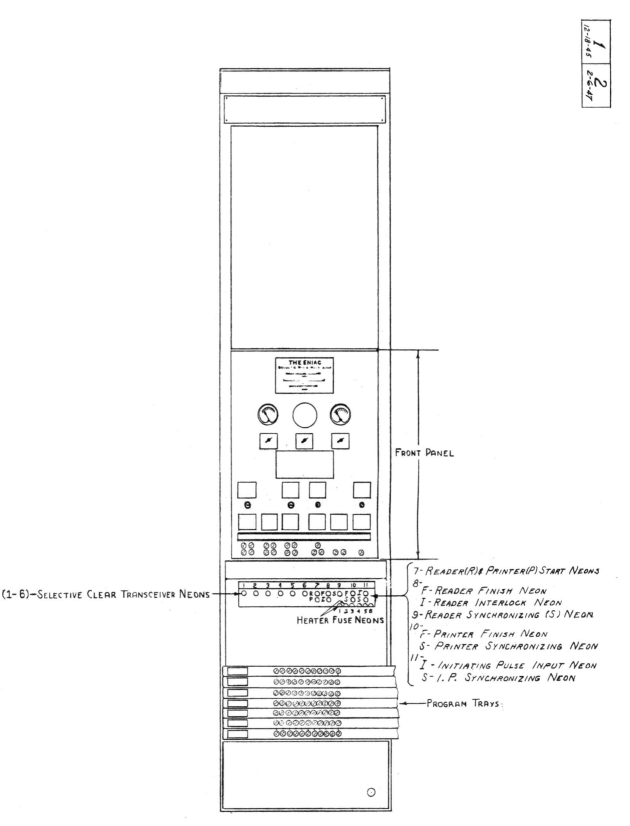

THE ENIAC

FRONT PANEL

7- READER(R) & PRINTER(P) START NEONS

(1-6)—SELECTIVE CLEAR TRANSCEIVER NEONS

8-
   F- READER FINISH NEON
   I- READER INTERLOCK NEON
9- READER SYNCHRONIZING (S) NEON
10-
   F- PRINTER FINISH NEON
   S- PRINTER SYNCHRONIZING NEON
11-
   I- INITIATING PULSE INPUT NEON
   S- I.P. SYNCHRONIZING NEON

HEATER FUSE NEONS

PROGRAM TRAYS

MOORE SCHOOL of ELECTRICAL ENGINEERING
UNIVERSITY of PENNSYLVANIA

INITIATING
UNIT
FRONT VIEW
PX-9-305

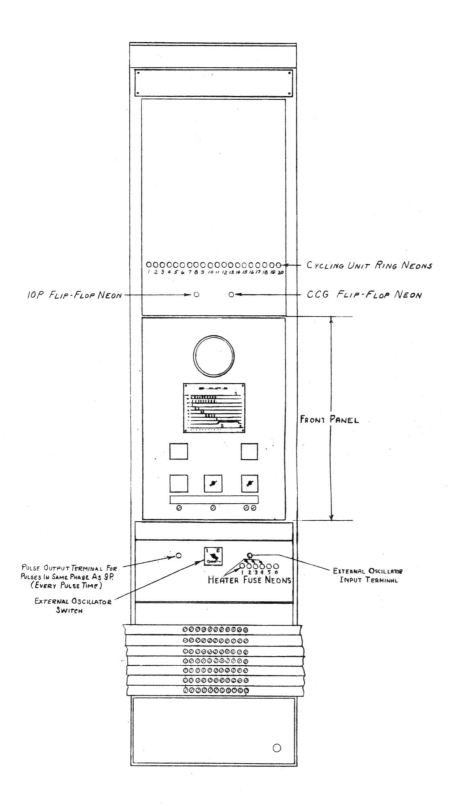

Cycling Unit Ring Neons

10P Flip-Flop Neon

CCG Flip-Flop Neon

Front Panel

Pulse Output Terminal For Pulses In Same Phase As 9P. (Every Pulse Time)

External Oscillator Switch

Heater Fuse Neons

External Oscillator Input Terminal

MOORE SCHOOL of ELECTRICAL ENGINEERING
UNIVERSITY of PENNSYLVANIA

CYCLING UNIT
FRONT VIEW
PX-9-304

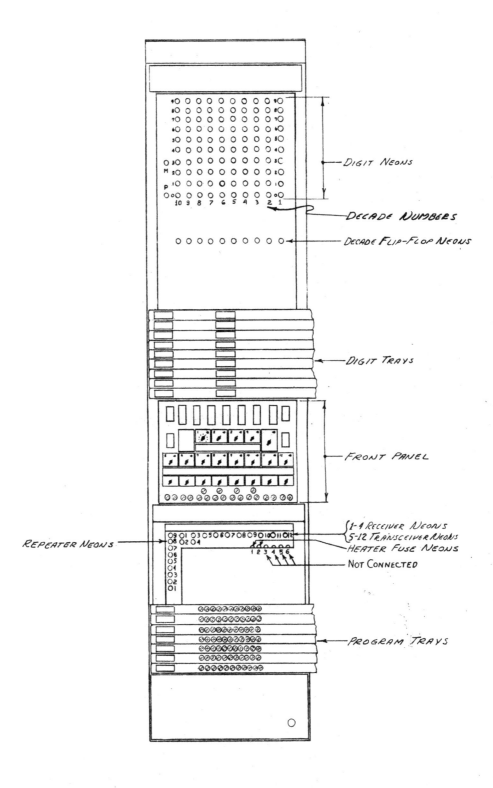

Digit Neons

Decade Numbers

Decade Flip-Flop Neons

Digit Trays

Front Panel

Repeater Neons

1-4 Receiver Neons
5-12 Transceiver Neons
Heater Fuse Neons
Not Connected

Program Trays

ACCUMULATOR
FRONT VIEW
PX-5-305

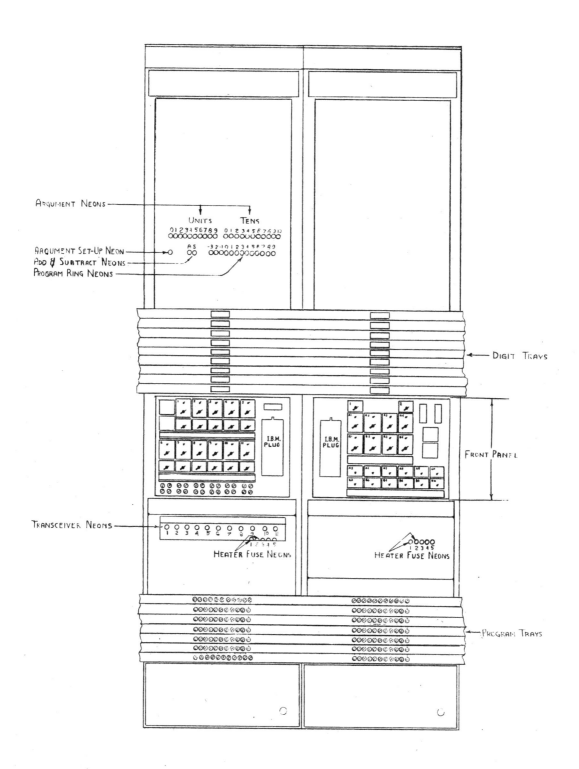

ARGUMENT NEONS

UNITS TENS
0123456789 0123456789

ARGUMENT SET-UP NEON
ADD & SUBTRACT NEONS
PROGRAM RING NEONS

AS -3-2-1 0 1 2 3 4 5 6 7 8 9 9

I.B.M. PLUG

I.B.M. PLUG

DIGIT TRAYS

FRONT PANEL

TRANSCEIVER NEONS
1 2 3 4 5 6 7 8 9 10 11
1 2 3 4 5
HEATER FUSE NEONS

1 2 3 4 5
HEATER FUSE NEONS

PROGRAM TRAYS

MOORE SCHOOL of ELECTRICAL ENGINEERING
UNIVERSITY of PENNSYLVANIA

FUNCTION
TABLE
FRONT VIEW
PX-7-305

NEONS ON DURING DIVISION

ADD. TIME	PROG. RING	PLACE RING	RECEIVER	1	2	3	D'_γ 4	N_γ 5	6	7	D 8	N^- 9	N^+ 10
I–1	A	9		①					ON	ON	ON		ON
2	B	9		ON					ON	ON	②		③
3	1	9		"					ON		"		"
II–1	A	i*	D_A or D_S	"					ON	ON	"		③
2	A	i	−1 or +1, Q_α	"						ON	"		"
S {1	A	Cycles	N_{AC}, S_α	"				ON		ON	"		"
S {2	A	i−1	S_{AC}, N'_γ	"						ON	"		Cycles
III 1	A	10−ρ	N_{AC}, S_α	"				ON			"		③
2	B	"	S_{AC}, N'_γ	"							"		Cycles
3	1	"	D_S or D_A	"			ON				"		③
4	2	"	D_S or D_A	"			ON				"		"
5	3	"	D_S or D_A	"			ON				"		"
6	4	"	D_S or D_A	"			ON				"		"
7	5	"	D_S or D_A	"			ON				"		"
8	6	"		"							"		"
9	7	"	(+1 or −1, Q_α)**	"							"		"
IV–1	7	"		"		④		⑤			"		
2	7	"		"		⑥	"				"		
TRANS-CEIVER OFF	A	9	1,2, or NEITHER	ON					ON	ON	ON		ON

NEONS ON DURING SQUARE ROOTING

ADD. TIME	PROG. RING	PLACE RING	RECEIVER	1	2	3	D'_γ 4	N_γ 5	6	7	D 8	N^- 9	N^+ 10
I–1	A	9		①					ON	ON	ON		ON
2	B	9							ON	ON	"		ON
3	1	9							ON	ON	"		ON
4	A	9	D_γ, +1						ON		"		ON
II–1	A	i*	D_S or D_A						ON	ON	"		③
2	A	i	+2 or −2D_γ							ON	"		"
S {1	A	Cycles	−1 or +1 S_α, N_{AC}					ON		ON	"		"
S {2	A	i−1	−1 or +1 N'_γ, S_{AC}					ON		ON	"		Cycles
III–1	A	10−ρ	−1 or +1, S_α, N_{AC}					ON			"		③
2	B	"	N'_γ, S_{AC}								"		Cycles
3	1	"	D_A or D_S				ON				"		③
4	2	"	D_A or D_S				ON				"		"
5	3	"	D_A or D_S				ON				"		"
6	4	"	D_A or D_S				ON				"		"
7	5	"	D_A or D_S				ON				"		"
8	6	"									"		"
9	7	"	(−2 or +2, D_γ)**								"		"
IV–1	7	"				④		⑤			"		"
2	7	"				⑥	"				"		"
TRANS-CEIVER OFF	A	9	3,4, or NEITHER						ON	ON	ON		ON

FOOT NOTES

① ON IF PREVIOUS PROGRAM WAS A DIVISION.
② ON IF DENOMINATOR IS POSITIVE WHEN RECEIVED IN DENOMINATOR ACCUMULATOR.
③ IF BEFORE DENOMINATOR IS ADDED TO OR SUBTRACTED FROM NUMERATOR, THE NUMERATOR IS POSITIVE, NEON #4 IS ON; OTHERWISE NEON #3 IS ON.
④ GOES ON WHEN INTERLOCK PULSE IS RECEIVED.
⑤ GOES ON ONE ADDITION TIME AFTER III–9.
⑥ GOES ON: a– IN NI CASE, TWO ADDITION TIMES AFTER III–9.
  b– IN I CASE, IN WHICHEVER OCCURS LATER: TWO ADDITION TIMES AFTER III–9 OR ONE ADDITION TIME AFTER NEON 7.
* $9 \geqq i \geqq 10-\rho$ WHERE ρ IS THE SETTING OF THE PLACES SWITCH.
** ONLY IF NO OVERDRAFT RESULTS.

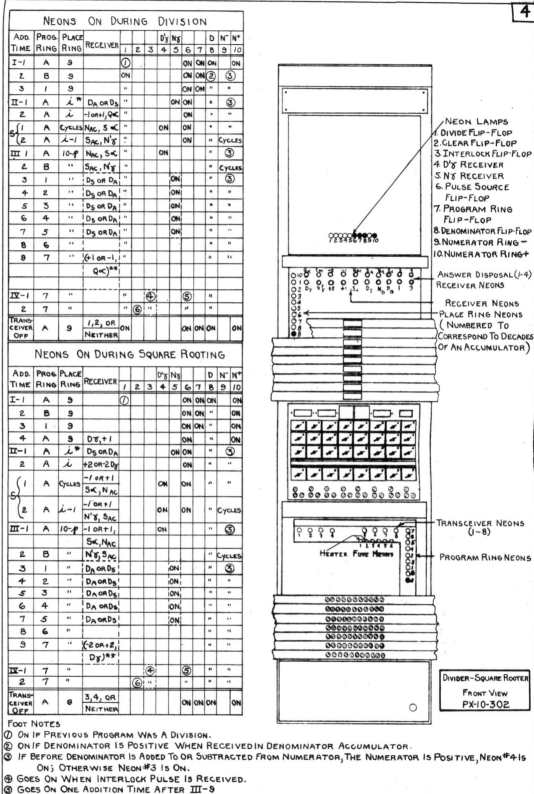

NEON LAMPS
1. DIVIDE FLIP-FLOP
2. CLEAR FLIP-FLOP
3. INTERLOCK FLIP-FLOP
4. D'_γ RECEIVER
5. N_γ RECEIVER
6. PULSE SOURCE FLIP-FLOP
7. PROGRAM RING FLIP-FLOP
8. DENOMINATOR FLIP-FLOP
9. NUMERATOR RING −
10. NUMERATOR RING +

ANSWER DISPOSAL (1-4) RECEIVER NEONS

RECEIVER NEONS PLACE RING NEONS (NUMBERED TO CORRESPOND TO DECADES OF AN ACCUMULATOR)

TRANSCEIVER NEONS (1-8)

HEATER FUSE NEONS

PROGRAM RING NEONS

DIVIDER–SQUARE ROOTER
FRONT VIEW
PX-10-302

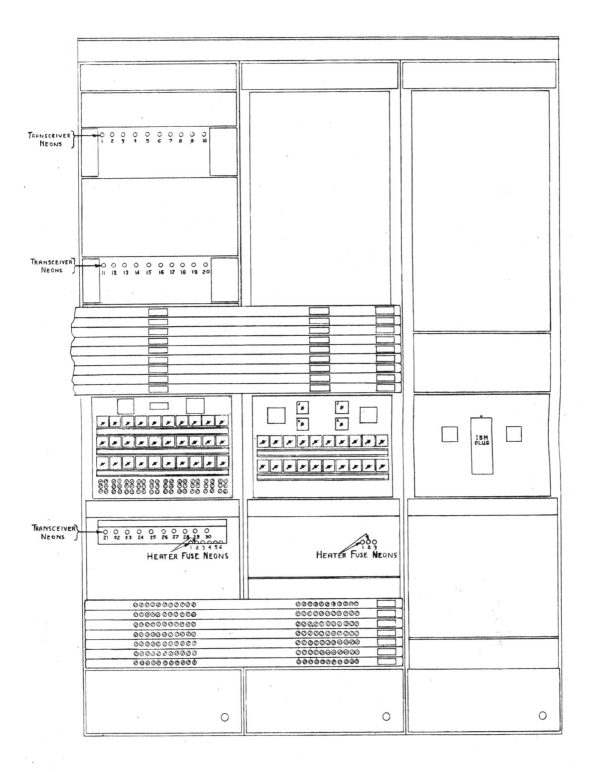

TRANSCEIVER NEONS
1 2 3 4 5 6 7 8 9 10

TRANSCEIVER NEONS
11 12 13 14 15 16 17 18 19 20

IBM PLUG

TRANSCEIVER NEONS
21 22 23 24 25 26 27 28 29 30
1 2 3 4 5 6
HEATER FUSE NEONS

1 2 3
HEATER FUSE NEONS

MOORE SCHOOL of ELECTRICAL ENGINEERING
UNIVERSITY of PENNSYLVANIA

CONSTANT
TRANSMITTER
FRONT VIEW
PX-11-306

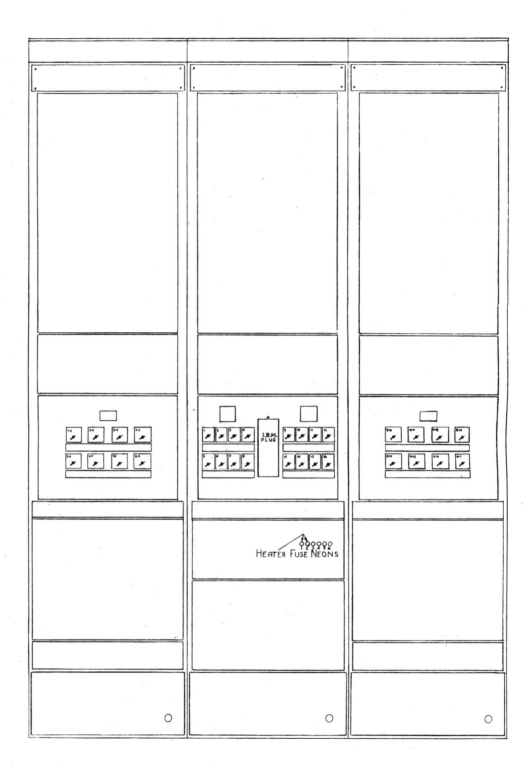

HEATER FUSE NEONS

I.B.M. PLUG

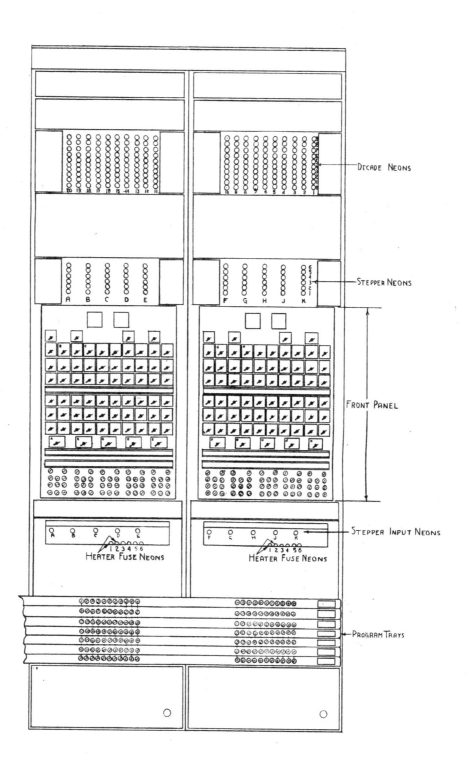

DECADE NEONS

STEPPER NEONS

FRONT PANEL

STEPPER INPUT NEONS

HEATER FUSE NEONS

HEATER FUSE NEONS

PROGRAM TRAYS

MOORE SCHOOL of ELECTRICAL ENGINEERING
UNIVERSITY of PENNSYLVANIA

MASTER
PROGRAMMER
FRONT VIEW
PX-8-303

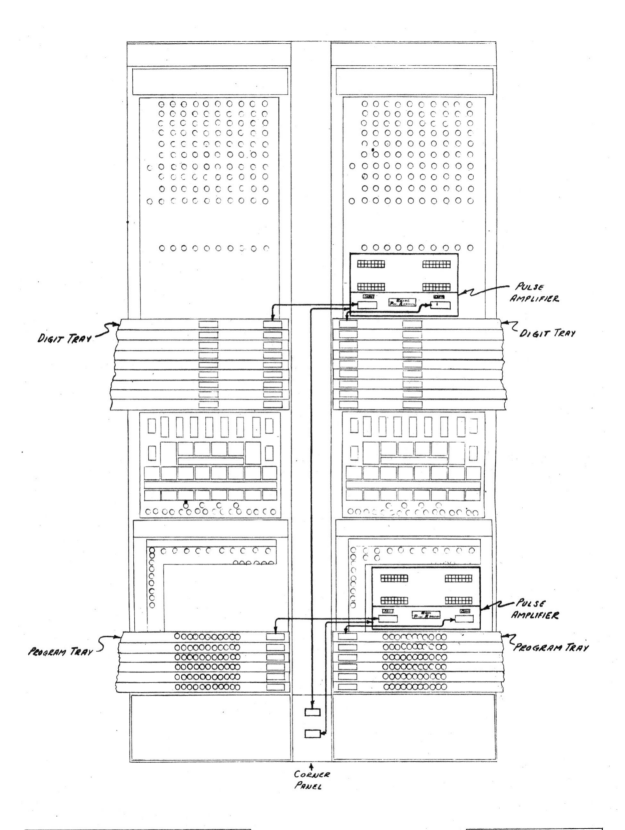

DIGIT TRAY

DIGIT TRAY

PULSE
AMPLIFIER

PROGRAM TRAY

PROGRAM TRAY

PULSE
AMPLIFIER

CORNER
PANEL

MOORE SCHOOL OF ELECTRICAL ENGINEERING
UNIVERSITY OF PENNSYLVANIA

PULSE AMPLIFIER
INTERCONNECTION DIAGRAM
PX-4-302

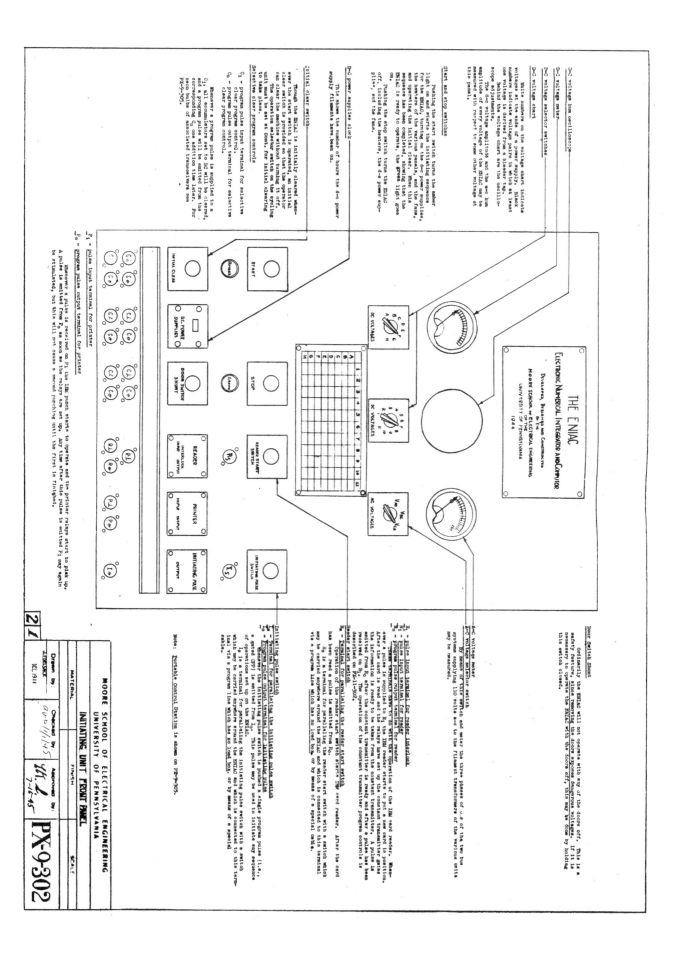

INITIATING UNIT FRONT PANEL

MOORE SCHOOL OF ELECTRICAL ENGINEERING
UNIVERSITY OF PENNSYLVANIA

PX-9-302

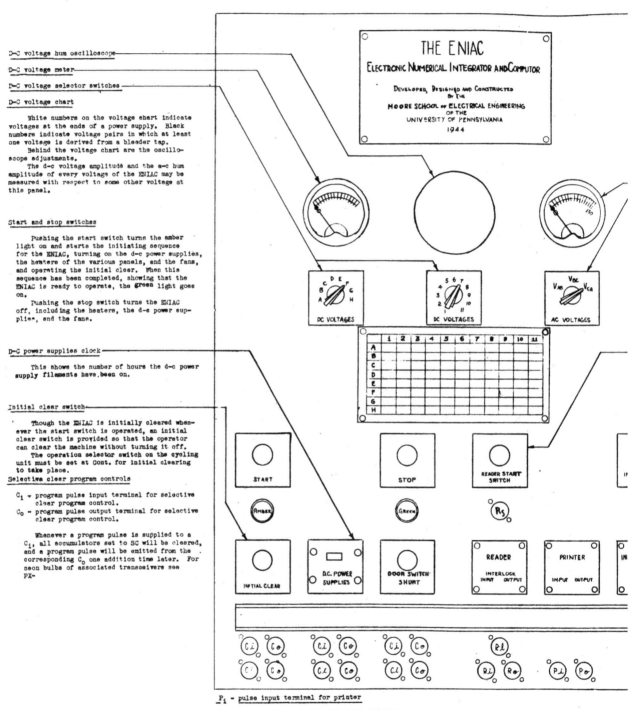

D-C voltage hum oscilloscope

D-C voltage meter

D-C voltage selector switches

D-C voltage chart

White numbers on the voltage chart indicate
voltages at the ends of a power supply. Black
numbers indicate voltage pairs in which at least
one voltage is derived from a bleeder tap.

Behind the voltage chart are the oscilloscope adjustments.

The d-c voltage amplitude and the a-c hum
amplitude of every voltage of the ENIAC may be
measured with respect to some other voltage at
this panel.

Start and stop switches

Pushing the start switch turns the amber
light on and starts the initiating sequence
for the ENIAC, turning on the d-c power supplies,
the heaters of the various panels, and the fans,
and operating the initial clear. When this
sequence has been completed, showing that the
ENIAC is ready to operate, the green light goes
on.

Pushing the stop switch turns the ENIAC
off, including the heaters, the d-c power supplies, and the fans.

D-C power supplies clock

This shows the number of hours the d-c power
supply filaments have been on.

Initial clear switch

Though the ENIAC is initially cleared whenever the start switch is operated, an initial
clear switch is provided so that the operator
can clear the machine without turning it off.

The operation selector switch on the cycling
unit must be set at Cont. for initial clearing
to take place.

Selective clear program controls

C_i - program pulse input terminal for selective
clear program control.
C_o - program pulse output terminal for selective
clear program control.

Whenever a program pulse is supplied to a
C_i, all accumulators set to SC will be cleared,
and a program pulse will be emitted from the
corresponding C_o one addition time later. For
neon bulbs of associated transceivers see
PX-

P_i - pulse input terminal for printer

P_o - program pulse output terminal for printer

Whenever a pulse is received on Pi the IBM punch starts to operate and the printer relays start t
A pulse is emitted from P_o as soon as the relays are set up. Any time after this pulse is emitted Pi
be stimulated, but this will not cause a second punching until the first is finished.

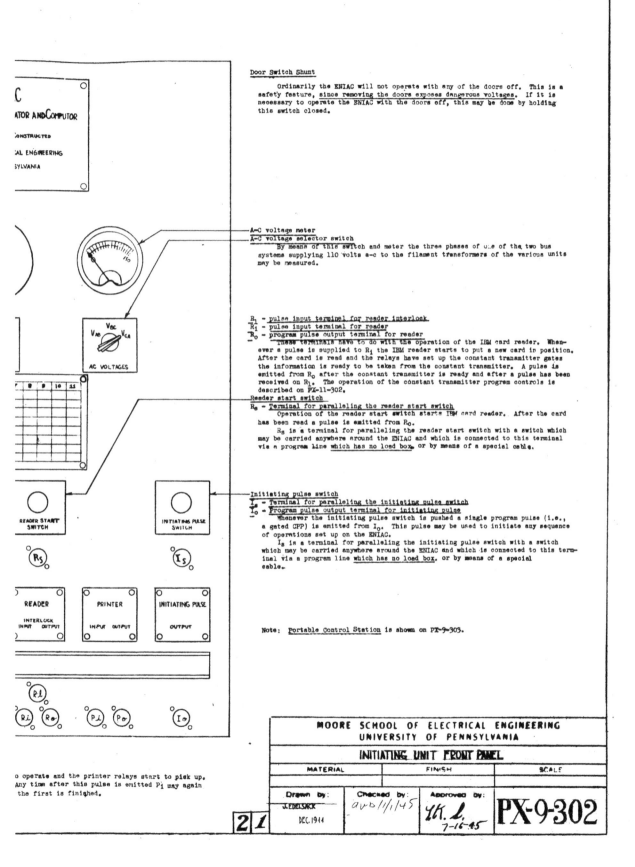

Door Switch Shunt

Ordinarily the ENIAC will not operate with any of the doors off. This is a safety feature, since removing the doors exposes dangerous voltages. If it is necessary to operate the ENIAC with the doors off, this may be done by holding this switch closed.

A-C voltage meter
A-C voltage selector switch

By means of this switch and meter the three phases of one of the two bus systems supplying 110 volts a-c to the filament transformers of the various units may be measured.

R_1 - pulse input terminal for reader interlock
R_i - pulse input terminal for reader
R_o - program pulse output terminal for reader

These terminals have to do with the operation of the IBM card reader. Whenever a pulse is supplied to R_i the IBM reader starts to put a new card in position. After the card is read and the relays have set up the constant transmitter gates the information is ready to be taken from the constant transmitter. A pulse is emitted from R_o after the constant transmitter is ready and after a pulse has been received on R_1. The operation of the constant transmitter program controls is described on PX-11-302.

Reader start switch
R_s - Terminal for paralleling the reader start switch

Operation of the reader start switch starts IBM card reader. After the card has been read a pulse is emitted from R_o.

R_s is a terminal for paralleling the reader start switch with a switch which may be carried anywhere around the ENIAC and which is connected to this terminal via a program line which has no load box, or by means of a special cable.

Initiating pulse switch
I_s - Terminal for paralleling the initiating pulse switch
I_o - Program pulse output terminal for initiating pulse

Whenever the initiating pulse switch is pushed a single program pulse (i.e., a gated CPP) is emitted from I_o. This pulse may be used to initiate any sequence of operations set up on the ENIAC.

I_s is a terminal for paralleling the initiating pulse switch with a switch which may be carried anywhere around the ENIAC and which is connected to this terminal via a program line which has no load box, or by means of a special cable.

Note: Portable Control Station is shown on PX-9-303.

o operate and the printer relays start to pick up.
Any time after this pulse is emitted P_i may again
the first is finished.

MOORE SCHOOL OF ELECTRICAL ENGINEERING		
UNIVERSITY OF PENNSYLVANIA		
INITIATING UNIT FRONT PANEL		
MATERIAL	FINISH	SCALE
Drawn by: J. EDELSACK DEC. 1944	Checked by: avo 11/1/45	Approved by: 7-16-45	PX-9-302

2 1

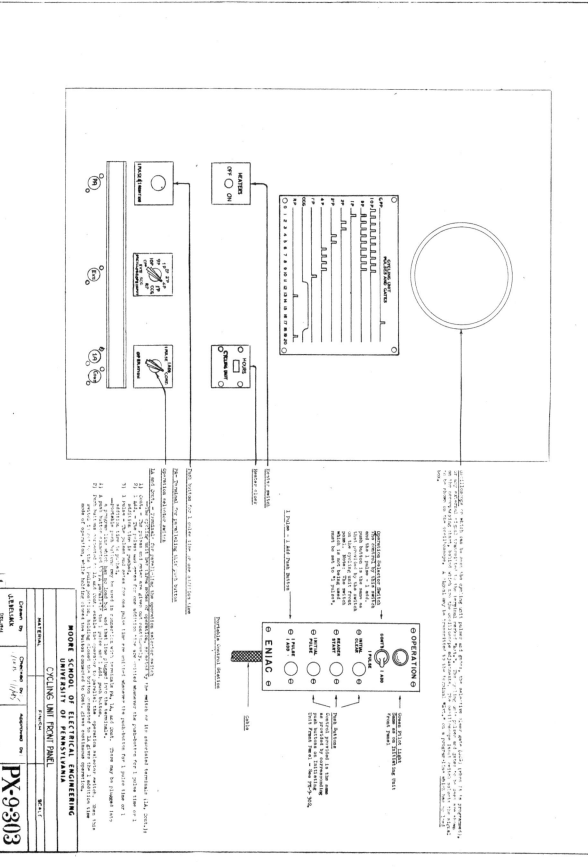

MOORE SCHOOL OF ELECTRICAL ENGINEERING
UNIVERSITY OF PENNSYLVANIA

CYCLING UNIT FRONT PANEL

Drawn by
J.E.BELSKIK
DEC.1944

Checked by

Approved by

MATERIAL

FINISH

SCALE

PX-9-303

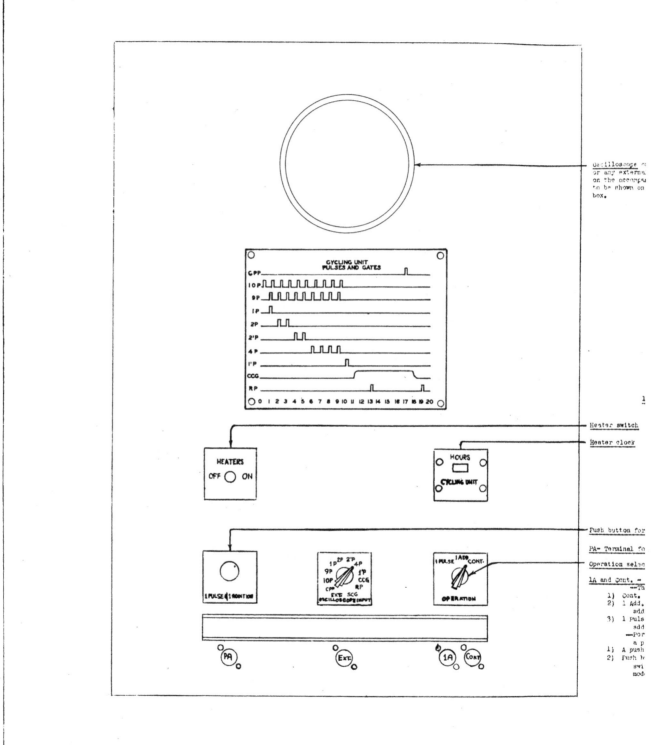

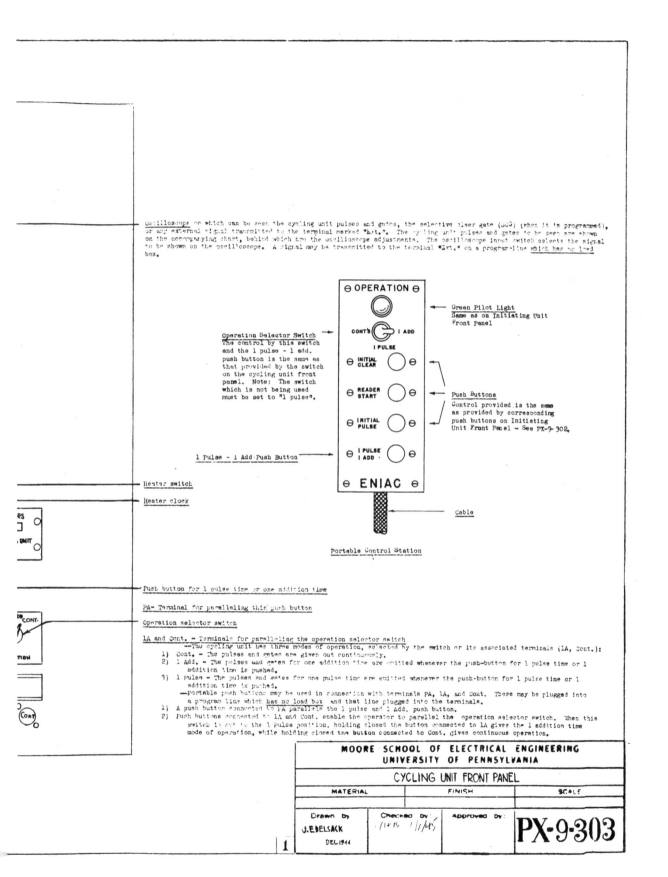

Oscilloscope on which can be seen the cycling unit pulses and gates, the selective clear gate (SCG) (when it is programmed), or any external signal transmitted to the terminal marked "Ext.". The cycling unit pulses and gates to be seen are shown on the accompanying chart, behind which are the oscilloscope adjustments. The oscilloscope input switch selects the signal to be shown on the oscilloscope. A signal may be transmitted to the terminal "Ext." on a program line which has no load box.

Green Pilot Light
Same as on Initiating Unit Front Panel

Operation Selector Switch
The control by this switch and the 1 pulse - 1 add. push button is the same as that provided by the switch on the cycling unit front panel. Note: The switch which is not being used must be set to "1 pulse".

Push Buttons
Control provided is the same as provided by corresponding push buttons on Initiating Unit Front Panel - See PX-9-302.

1 Pulse - 1 Add-Push Button

Cable

Portable Control Station

Heater switch

Heater clock

Push button for 1 pulse time or one addition time

PA- Terminal for paralleling this push button

Operation selector switch

1A and Cont. - Terminals for paralleling the operation selector switch
    —The cycling unit has three modes of operation, selected by the switch or its associated terminals (1A, Cont.):
1) Cont. - The pulses and gates are given out continuously.
2) 1 Add. - The pulses and gates for one addition time are emitted whenever the push-button for 1 pulse time or 1 addition time is pushed.
3) 1 Pulse - The pulses and gates for one pulse time are emitted whenever the push-button for 1 pulse time or 1 addition time is pushed.
    —Portable push buttons may be used in connection with terminals PA, 1A, and Cont. These may be plugged into a program line which has no load box and that line plugged into the terminals.
1) A push button connected to PA parallels the 1 pulse and 1 Add. push button.
2) Push buttons connected to 1A and Cont. enable the operator to parallel the operation selector switch. When this switch is set to the 1 Pulse position, holding closed the button connected to 1A gives the 1 addition time mode of operation, while holding closed the button connected to Cont. gives continuous operation.

MOORE SCHOOL OF ELECTRICAL ENGINEERING UNIVERSITY OF PENNSYLVANIA			
CYCLING UNIT FRONT PANEL			
MATERIAL		FINISH	SCALE
Drawn by J.EDELSACK DEC 1944	Checked by: //WB 1/1/45	Approved by:	PX-9-303

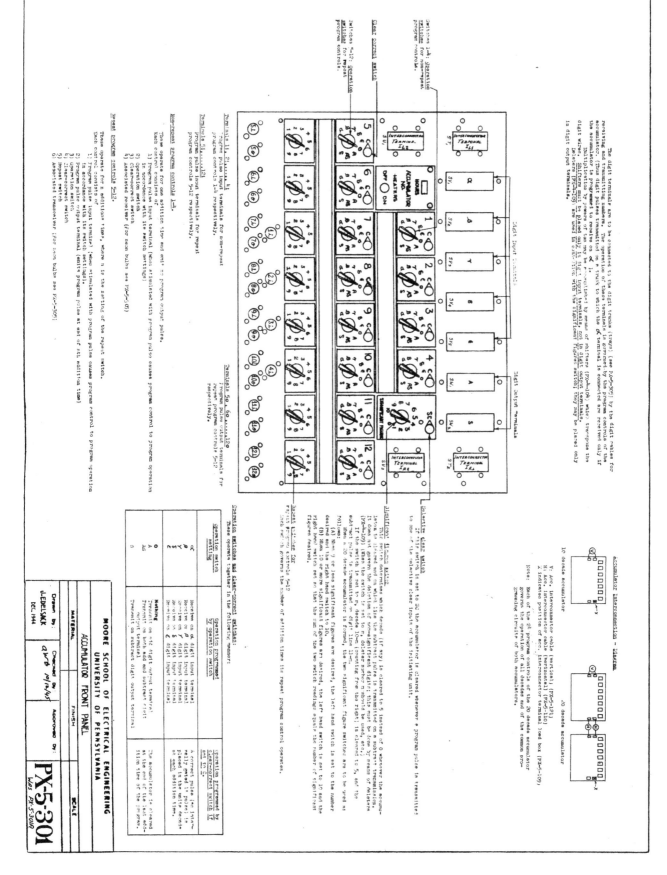

MOORE SCHOOL OF ELECTRICAL ENGINEERING
UNIVERSITY OF PENNSYLVANIA

ACCUMULATOR FRONT PANEL

PX-5-301

The digit terminals are to be connected to the digit trunks (trays) (see PX-5-305) by the digit cables for receiving and transmitting numbers. The operation of these terminals is governed by the program controls of the accumulator. (Thus digit pulses transmitted on a trunk to which the α terminal is connected are received only if the accumulator is programmed to receive on α).

Multiplication by powers of ten may be accomplished by means of shifters (PX-4-104) which transpose the digit wires. Shifters must be placed only in digit input terminals, not in digit output terminals.

Deleters (PX-4-109) are used in connection with the significant figures switch; they may be placed only in digit output terminals.

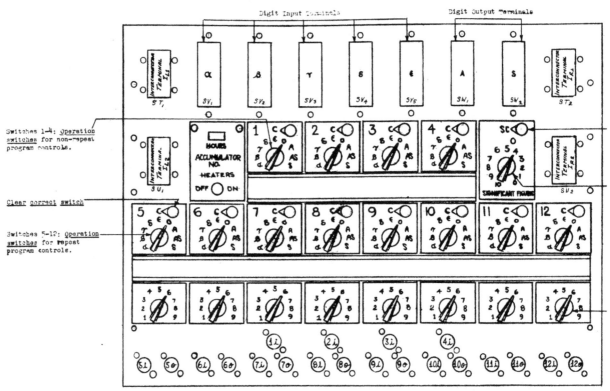

Terminals 1i, 2i,..... 4i
    Program pulse input terminals for non-repeat program controls 1-4 respectively.

Terminals 5o, 6o 12o
    Program pulse output terminals for repeat program controls 5-12 respectively.

Terminals 5i,.....12i
    Program pulse input terminals for repeat program controls 5-12 respectively.

Non-repeat program controls 1-4.

    These operate for one addition time and emit no program output pulses.
    Each control consists of
        1) Program pulse input terminal (when stimulated with program pulse causes program control to program operation in accordance with its switch settings)
        2) Operation switch
        3) Clear-correct switch
        4) Associated receiver (For neon bulbs see PX-5-305)

Repeat program controls 5-12.

    These operate for n additions times, where n is the setting of the repeat switch.
    Each control consists of
        1) Program pulse input terminal (when stimulated with program pulse causes program control to program operation in accordance with its switch settings).
        2) Program pulse output terminal (emits program pulse at end of nth addition time)
        3) Operation switch
        4) Clear-correct switch
        5) Repeat switch
        6) Associated transceiver (For neon bulbs see PX-5-305)

-5-305) by the digit cables for
the program controls of the
onnected are received only if

X-4-104) which transpose the
tput terminals.
tch; they may be placed only

Accumulator Interconnection - Diagram

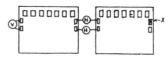

10 decade accumulator   20 decade accumulator

V: Acc. interconnector cable (vertical) (PX-5-121)
H: Acc. interconnector cable (horizontal) (PX-5-110)
X indicates position of acc. interconnector terminal load box (PX-5-109)

Note: Each of the 2^4 program controls of the 20 decade accumulator
governs the operation of all decades and of the common programming circuits of both accumulators.

git Output Terminals

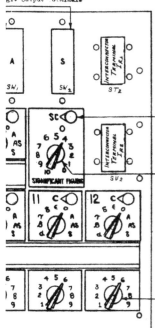

Selective clear switch

If this switch is set to SC the accumulator is cleared whenever a program pulse is transmitted
to one of the selective clear inputs of the initiating unit.

Significant figures switch

This switch determines which decade (if any) is cleared to 5 instead of 0 whenever the accumu-
lator is cleared and on which line the subtract pulse is transmitted on a subtract transmission.
It does not govern the deletion of non-significant digits; this must be done by means of deleters
(PX-4-109) (When the switch is set to m, deleter number m should be used, etc.)

If the switch is set to m, decade 10-m (counting from the right) is cleared to 5, and the
subtract pulse is transmitted on digit line 11-m.

When a 20 decade accumulator is formed, the two significant figure switches are to be used as
follows:

(A) When 9 or less significant figures are desired, the left hand switch is set to the number
desired and the right hand switch to 10.

(B) When 10 or more significant figures are desired, the left hand switch is set to 10 and the
right hand switch set so that the sum of the two switch readings equals the number of significant
figures desired.

Repeat switches for
repeat program controls 5-12

Each switch governs the number of addition times its repeat program control operates.

inals 5o, 6o.....12o
Program pulse output terminals for
repeat program controls 5-12
respectively.

Operation switches and clear-correct switches:

These operate together in the following manner:

Operation switch setting	Operation programmed by operation switch	Operation programmed by clear-correct switch if set to C.
α β γ δ ε	Receive on α digit input terminal Receive on β digit input terminal Receive on γ digit input terminal Receive on δ digit input terminal Receive on ε digit input terminal	A correct pulse (an inter- nally gated 1' pulse) is placed in the units decade at each addition time.
O A AS S	Nothing Transmit on add digit output terminal Transmit on both add and subtract digit output terminal Transmit on subtract digit output terminal	The accumulator is cleared at the end of the last add- ition time of the program.

s program control to program operation

s program control to program operation

(on time)

<table>
<tr><td colspan="4">MOORE SCHOOL OF ELECTRICAL ENGINEERING
UNIVERSITY OF PENNSYLVANIA</td></tr>
<tr><td colspan="4">ACCUMULATOR FRONT PANEL</td></tr>
<tr><td>MATERIAL</td><td>FINISH</td><td colspan="2">SCALE</td></tr>
<tr><td>Drawn by:
J. EDELSACK
DEC. 1944</td><td>Checked by:
aWB 10/12/45</td><td>Approved by:</td><td>PX-5-301
Was PX-5-301A</td></tr>
</table>

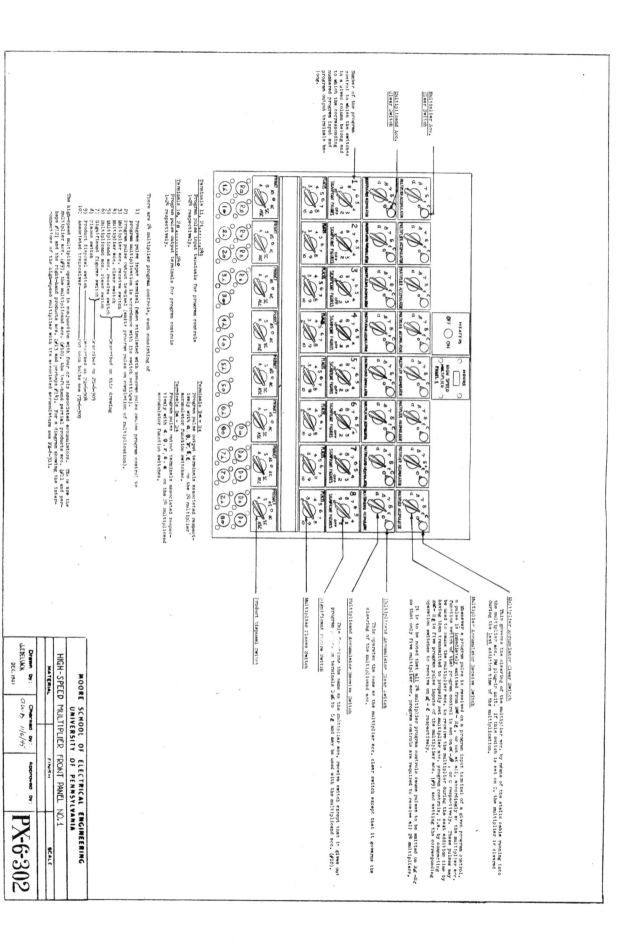

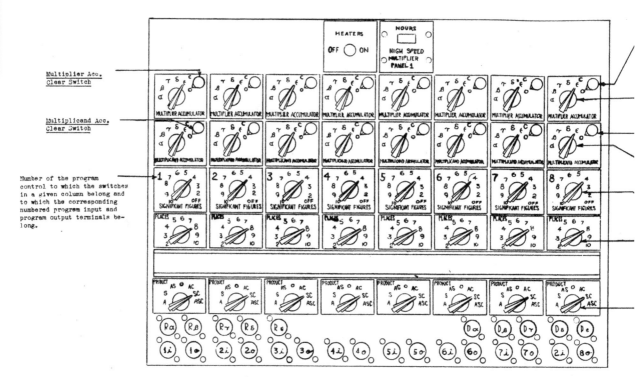

Multiplier Acc.
Clear Switch

Multiplicand Acc.
Clear Switch

Number of the program
control to which the switches
in a given column belong and
to which the corresponding
numbered program input and
program output terminals belong.

Terminals 1i, 2i,......,24i
    Program pulse input terminals for program controls
    1-24 respectively.

Terminals 1o, 2o........,24o
    Program pulse output terminals for program controls
    1-24 respectively.

Terminals Rα - Rε
    Program pulse output terminals associated respect-
    ively with α, β, γ, δ, ε on the 24 multiplier
    accumulator function switches.

Terminals Dα - Dε
    Program pulse output terminals associated respec-
    tively with α, β, γ, δ, ε on the 24 multiplicand
    accumulator function switches.

There are 24 multiplier program controls, each consisting of

    1) Program pulse input terminal (when stimulated with program pulse causes program control to
       program multiplication in accordance with its switch settings).
    2) Program pulse output terminal (emits program pulse on completion of multiplication).
    3) Multiplier acc. receive switch
    4) Multiplier acc. clear switch
    5) Multiplicand acc. receive switch   Described on this drawing
    6) Multiplicand acc. clear switch
    7) Significant figures switch   Described on PX-6-303
    8) Places switch
    9) Product disposal switch   Described on PX-6-304
    10) Associated transceiver   For neon bulbs see PX-6-309

The high-speed multiplier operates in conjunction with four or six associated accumulators. These are the
    multiplier acc. (#9), the multiplicand acc. (#10), the left-hand partial products acc. (#11 and per-
    haps #12) and the right-hand products acc. (#13 and perhaps #14). For a diagram showing the inter-
    connections of the high-speed multiplier with its associated accumulators see PX-6-311.

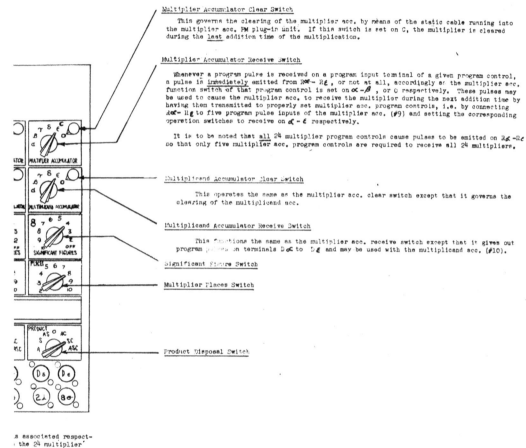

Multiplier Accumulator Clear Switch

This governs the clearing of the multiplier acc. by means of the static cable running into the multiplier acc. PM plug-in unit. If this switch is set on C, the multiplier is cleared during the last addition time of the multiplication.

Multiplier Accumulator Receive Switch

Whenever a program pulse is received on a program input terminal of a given program control, a pulse is immediately emitted from $R\alpha - R\epsilon$, or not at all, accordingly as the multiplier acc. function switch of that program control is set on $\alpha - \beta$, or O respectively. These pulses may be used to cause the multiplier acc. to receive the multiplier during the next addition time by having them transmitted to properly set multiplier acc. program controls, i.e. by connecting $R\alpha - 11\epsilon$ to five program pulse inputs of the multiplier acc. (#9) and setting the corresponding operation switches to receive on $\alpha - \epsilon$ respectively.

It is to be noted that all 24 multiplier program controls cause pulses to be emitted on $R\alpha - R\epsilon$ so that only five multiplier acc. program controls are required to receive all 24 multipliers.

Multiplicand Accumulator Clear Switch

This operates the same as the multiplier acc. clear switch except that it governs the clearing of the multiplicand acc.

Multiplicand Accumulator Receive Switch

This functions the same as the multiplier acc. receive switch except that it gives out program pulses on terminals $D\alpha$ to $D\epsilon$ and may be used with the multiplicand acc. (#10).

Significant Figure Switch

Multiplier Places Switch

Product Disposal Switch

s associated respect-
the 24 multiplier

s associated respec-
on the 24 multiplicand

to

se are the
l and per-
he inter-

MOORE SCHOOL OF ELECTRICAL ENGINEERING		
UNIVERSITY OF PENNSYLVANIA		
HIGH-SPEED MULTIPLIER FRONT PANEL NO. 1		
MATERIAL	FINISH	SCALE

Drawn by:	Checked by:	Approved by:	
J.EDELSACK	aub 11/6/45		PX-6-302
DEC. 1944			

Significant Figures Switch

This switch may be used to give a variable round-off; i.e., a product which is rounded off in a different places for each program channel. This switch governs the addition of 5 pulses into the proper place of the left-hand product acc. (#11, 12) during the second addition time of the multiplication.

It does not control the deletion of the non-significant digits of the product nor the placing of the significant pulses in the proper channel of the product on a subtract transmission. Since these vary with the setting of the significant figures switch, they must be taken care of at the accumulator which receives the product. Hence in cases where every product is to be rounded-off to the same number of places, it is best to use the round-off facilities of the right-hand product acc. (#13, 14).

Places Switch

This governs the number of places of the multiplier that are to be used in the multiplication. The multiplier digits are used from left to right, so that the most significant digits are used first. The places referred to are the places of the multiplier acc. counted from the left. The places switch is completely independent of the significant figures switch. The reason for this is that all digits of the multiplicand are used in the multiplication process. The only purpose of the places switch is to save time.

Time schedule for multiplication

A multiplication requires from 6 to 8 addition times (depending upon the setting of the places switch) including the time required for resetting the multiplier and multiplicand, but not including the time required for disposal of the product.

Addition time	Operation
(Program input pulse received at end of CB)	
1	Multiplier and multiplicand received
2	Five round-off pulses transmitted to left-hand product acc. (#11, 12)
3	Multiplicand multiplied by first place (10th decade) of multiplier and left and right place components transmitted to left and right hand product accs.
p+2	This is continued up to the p+2th addition time, where p setting of places switch
p+3	Complement corrections are made when necessary.
p+4	Accumulated left hand products are added into accumulated right hand products.
(Program output pulse and answer disposal pulse emitted at end of p+4th addition time)	

MOORE SCHOOL OF ELECTRICAL ENGINEERING
UNIVERSITY OF PENNSYLVANIA

HIGH-SPEED MULTIPLIER FRONT PANEL NO. 2

Drawn by:	Checked By:	Approved By:	PX-6-303
J.P. ECKERT			
DEC. 1944			
MATERIAL		FINISH	SCALE

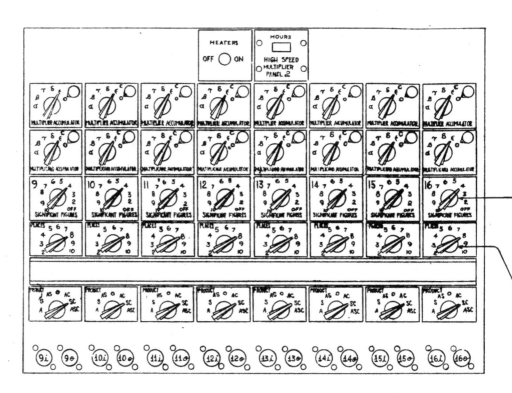

Time schedule for multiplication

    A multiplication requires from 6 to 14 addition times (depending upon the setting of the places switch) including the time required for receiving the multiplier and multiplicand, but not including the time required for disposal of the product.

Addition time	Operation
(Program input pulse received at end of 0th addition time)	
1	Multiplier and multiplicand received
2	Five round-off pulses transmitted to left-hand product acc. (#11, 12)
3	Multiplicand multiplied by first place (10th decade) of multiplier and left and right hand components transmitted to left and right hand product acc.
$p+2$	This is continued up to the $p+2$d addition time, where p setting of places switch
$p+3$	Complement corrections are made when necessary.
$p+4$	Accumulated left hand products are added into accumulated right hand products.
(Program output pulse and answer disposal pulse emitted at end of $p+4$th addition time)	

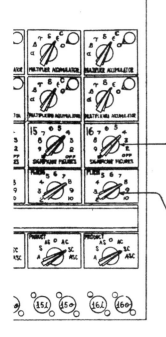

Significant Figures Switch

This switch may be used to give a variable round-off; i.e., a product which is rounded off in a different place for each program control. This switch governs the addition of 5 pulses into the proper place of the left-hand product acc. (#11, 12) during the second addition time of the multiplication.

It does not control the deletion of the non-significant digits of the product nor the placing of the subtract pulse in the proper channel of the product on a subtract transmission. Since these vary with the setting of the significant figures switch, they must be taken care of at the accumulator which receives the product. Hence in cases where every product is to be rounded-off to the same number of places, it is best to use the round-off facilities of the right-hand product acc. (#13, 14).

Places Switch

This governs the number of places of the multiplier that are to be used in the multiplication. The multiplier digits are used from left to right, so that the most significant digits are used first. The places referred to are the places of the multiplier acc. counted from the left.

The places switch is completely independent of the significant figures switch. The reason for this is that all digits of the multiplicand are used in the multiplication process. The only purpose of the places switch is to save time.

on the setting of the
and multiplicand, but

oft-hand product acc. (#11, 12)
(10th decade) of multiplier
emitted to left and right hand

tion time, where p setting of

cessary.
d into accumulated right hand

p+4th addition time)

| MOORE SCHOOL OF ELECTRICAL ENGINEERING |
| UNIVERSITY OF PENNSYLVANIA |

HIGH-SPEED MULTIPLIER FRONT PANEL NO. 2

MATERIAL	FINISH	SCALE

Drawn By:	Checked By:	Approved By:	
J. ZEBELSKK			PX-6-303
DEC. 1944			

MOORE SCHOOL OF ELECTRICAL ENGINEERING
UNIVERSITY OF PENNSYLVANIA

HIGH-SPEED MULTIPLIER FRONT PANEL NO. 3

Drawn By:	Checked By	Approved By	
J.EDELMAN DEC.1944			PX-6-304

| MATERIAL | | FINISH | SCALE |

1

These terminals are to be semi-permanently connected to the α digit input terminals (see note on terminals l,r) of the product accumulators (#11, 12, 13, 14) by trays or cables not used for any other purpose. No load boxes are to be used. The digit pulses emitted from these terminals are not supplied from transmitters, but from inverter tubes which cannot be connected in parallel with anything else and which have their own resistors. Hence the α digit input terminals of the product accumulators cannot be used for receiving any other numbers.

No shifters or deleters are to be used. Accumulators 11 and 12 and accumulators 13 and 14 are paired when more than eight places is desired in the product.

The load on these outputs must be kept as small as possible. Recommended method of connection is:

L.H. #1   By special cable to Accumulator 11.
L.H. #2   By short cable to tray (only one tray), and short cable to Accumulator 12.
R.H. #1   By special cable to Accumulator 13.
R.H. #2   Similar to L.H. #2 and Accumulator 12.

See also drawing PX-6-311

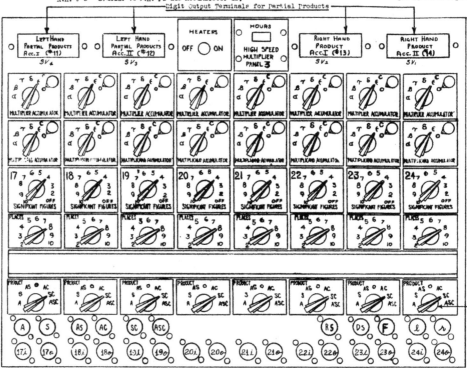

Digit Output Terminals for Partial Products

Terminals A-ASC
Program output terminals associated respectively with A, S, AS, AC, SC, ASC, on product disposal switch.

Terminals RS, DS, F
Program pulse output terminals for transmitting pulses used in the programming of each multiplication:

DS - A program pulse is emitted at the end of the p+2d addition time if the multiplier is negative. Semi-permanent connections must be established so that this pulse programs the multiplicand acc. to transmit subtract and the right hand product accumulator I(#13) to receive.

RS - A program pulse is emitted at the end of the p+2d addition time if the multiplicand is negative. Semi-permanent connections must be established so that this pulse programs the multiplier acc. (#9) to transmit subtract and the left hand partial products acc. I (#11) to receive.

F - A program pulse is emitted at the end of the p+3d addition time. Semi-permanent connections must be established so that this pulse programs the left hand partial products accumulator (#11, 12) to transmit add (without shifting) and clear and programs the right hand product accumulator (#13, 14) to receive, or vice-versa.

Terminals l,r
Receiver cathode follower buffer output lines. These are to be used to program the product acc. to receive the partial products. The following semi-permanent connections are to be established.
1. l is to be connected via acc. interconnector cable (Mult.) (PX-5-131) into the interconnector terminals I₁₁ and I₁₂ of left-hand partial products acc. I (#11). The α digit input terminal is to be used to receive the partial products.
2. r is to be similarly connected into right-hand product accumulator I (#13). Likewise, the α digit input terminal is to be used to receive the partial products.

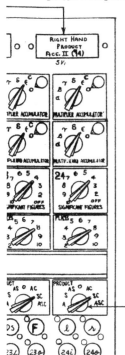

als (see note on terminals l,r)
purpose. No load boxes are to
~~rs~~, but from inverter tubes which
Hence the ⊄ digit input terminals

13 and 14 are paired when more

f connection is:

or 12.

See also drawing PX-6-311

itting pulses used in the

i of the p+2d addition time
anent connections must be
he multiplicand acc. to trans-
ccumulator I(#13) to receive.

i of the p+2d addition time
rmanent connections must be
he multiplier acc. (#9) to
al products acc. I (#11) to

of the p+3d addition time.
ished so that this pulse pro-
sulator (#11, 12) to transmit
rams the right hand product
-versa.

ines. These are to be used to
artial products. The following
plished.
aterconnector cable (Mult.)
tor terminals I_{11} and I_{12} of
I (#11). The ⊄ digit input
rs the partial products.
into right-hand product accumu-
digit input terminal is to be
ucts.

Product disposal switch

This switch operates in conjunction with program pulse output terminals A through ASC and provides program facilities for the disposal of all 24 products using at most 6 program controls of the right-hand product accumulator (#13, 14).

At the end of the p+4th addition time (i.e., at the same time as the program output pulse is emitted) a program pulse is emitted from A-ASC according to the setting of the product disposal switch of the program control being used.

Semi-permanent connections may be established by connecting A through ASC to six program pulse inputs of the right-hand product acc. (#13, 14) and setting the corresponding operation switches and clear-correct switches to transmit on A-ASC. The program control output pulse may be used to stimulate that unit of the ENIAC which is to receive the transmitted product.

MOORE SCHOOL OF ELECTRICAL ENGINEERING		
UNIVERSITY OF PENNSYLVANIA		
HIGH-SPEED MULTIPLIER FRONT PANEL NO. 3		
MATERIAL	FINISH	SCALE
Drawn by: J.LEBELSKI.K DEC.1944	Checked by:	Approved by:

PX-6-304

1

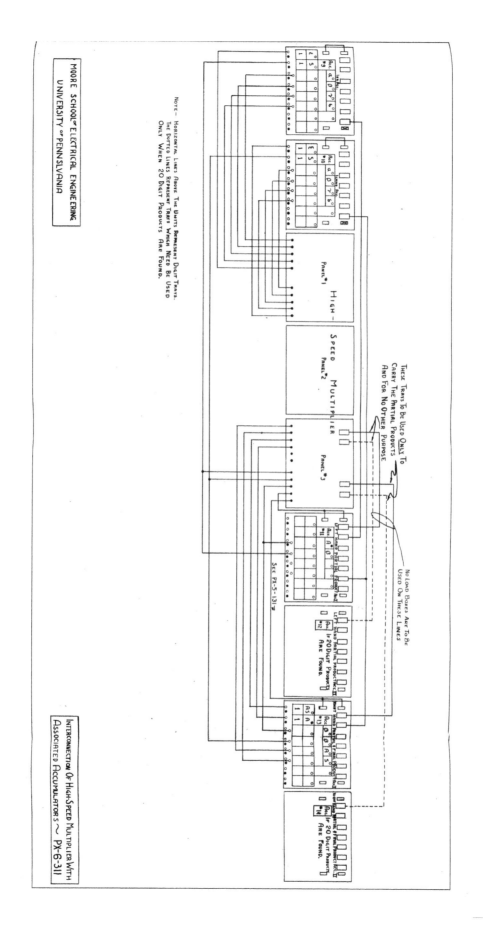

MOORE SCHOOL of ELECTRICAL ENGINEERING
UNIVERSITY of PENNSYLVANIA

NOTE— HORIZONTAL LINES ABOVE THE UNITS REPRESENT DIGIT TRAYS.
THE DOTTED LINES REPRESENT TRAYS WHICH NEED BE USED
ONLY WHEN 20 DIGIT PRODUCTS ARE FOUND.

INTERCONNECTION OF HIGH-SPEED MULTIPLIER WITH
ASSOCIATED ACCUMULATORS ~ PX-6-311

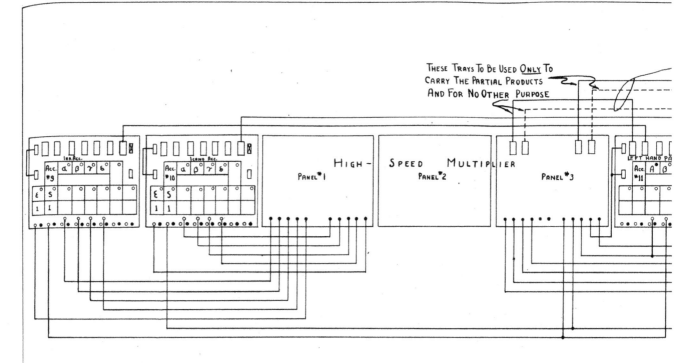

THESE TRAYS TO BE USED <u>ONLY</u> TO
CARRY THE PARTIAL PRODUCTS
AND FOR NO OTHER PURPOSE

HIGH - SPEED MULTIPLIER

PANEL #1   PANEL #2   PANEL #3

NOTE— HORIZONTAL LINES ABOVE THE UNITS REPRESENT DIGIT TRAYS.
THE DOTTED LINES REPRESENT TRAYS WHICH NEED BE USED
ONLY WHEN 20 DIGIT PRODUCTS ARE FOUND.

MOORE SCHOOL OF ELECTRICAL ENGINEERING
UNIVERSITY OF PENNSLVANIA

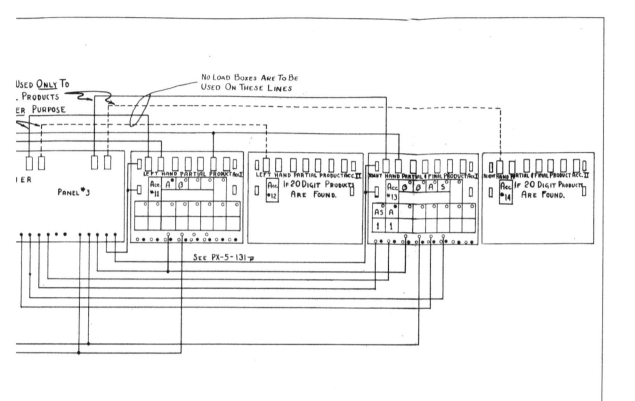

USED ONLY TO
. PRODUCTS
ER PURPOSE

NO LOAD BOXES ARE TO BE
USED ON THESE LINES

IER

PANEL #3

LEFT HAND PARTIAL PRODUCT ACC.I

Acc.
#11

A° A°

LEFT HAND PARTIAL PRODUCT ACC.II

Acc.
#12

IF 20 DIGIT PRODUCTS
ARE FOUND.

RIGHT HAND PARTIAL & FINAL PRODUCT ACC.I

Acc.
#13

A° A° A° S

AS A°

1 1

RIGHT HAND PARTIAL & FINAL PRODUCT ACC.II

Acc.
#14

IF 20 DIGIT PRODUCTS
ARE FOUND.

SEE PX-5-131

INTERCONNECTION OF HIGH-SPEED MULTIPLIER WITH
ASSOCIATED ACCUMULATORS ∼ PX-6-311

Argument input terminal

This input is open for reception of the two-digit argument during the 2nd addition time of operation 10A. The units place is received on line 1, the tens place on line 2. Differences (0pal-10) should be able to shift the argument if it opens from other devices than the T.B. and G.G. The other lines of this terminal are unconnected, so a deleter is not required.

The memorizer which transmits the argument may be programmed from terminals NC and C.

The function note automatically clears its argument at the end of each operation.

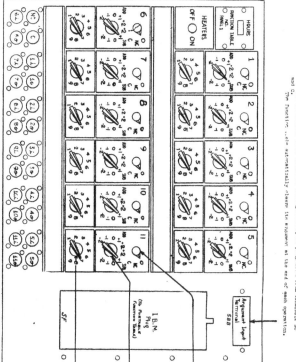

Argument reception switch

This switch operates in conjunction with program pulse output terminals NC and C and may be used to program an accumulator or accumulators to transmit the argument which is set on NC or C respectively. Semi-permanent connections may be established by connecting NC and C to program input terminals of the argument accumulator and setting the corresponding operation switches to transmit and transmit-and-clear respectively.

There are eleven program controls on each function table. Each program control consists of a program pulse input terminal (which, when stimulated with a program pulse, causes the program control to program the function value), a program pulse output terminal (which emits a pulse on completion of the operation), the three switches described below, and an associated transmitter (for neon bulbs see PX-7-305).

Operation switch

This switch determines whether the function value (add) or its complement (subtract) is transmitted. It also determines whether the function value of one of the neighboring arguments is transmitted. Thus positions-2, -1, 0, +1, +2 give f(n-2), f(n-1), f(n), f(n+1), f(n+2) respectively, where n is the argument.

Operation repeat switch

This switch determines the number of times the function value is transmitted.

Note that 4 addition times are required for the function value to set up, receive the argument, etc. This loss of time must be taken account of in programming the accumulator which receives the value of the function. Thus if that accumulator is programmed with the same pulse that programs the function, it could receive the value of the function only 5 times.

MATERIAL				
Drawn by: J.FRENK FEB.1944	Checked by: a.v.b 10/25/45	Approved by:		PX-7-302

MOORE SCHOOL OF ELECTRICAL ENGINEERING
UNIVERSITY OF PENNSYLVANIA
FUNCTION TABLE FRONT PANEL No.1

1

Terminals 1A, 2A.....11A
Program pulse input terminals for program control 1-11 respectively

Terminals 1o 2o......11o
Program pulse output terminals for program controls 1-11 respectively

Terminal NC
Program pulse output terminal associated with NC on argument reception switch.

Terminal C
Program pulse output terminal associated with C on argument reception switch.

Time Schedule for Function Table

Addition time
(program input pulse received at end of nth addition time)

	Operation
1	Circuits set up
2	Argument received
3	Argument modified by the addition of 0 to 4 pulses. At the pulse time p-value function table starts
4	Function table firstbare setting up
5	Value of function transmitted
	This is continued up to the r+4-th addition time, where r is the setting of the function repeat switch.

(r+5)-th: no output emitted at end of r+4-th addition time)

<u>Argument input terminal</u>

This input is open for reception of the two-digit argument during the 2nd addition time of operation. The units place is received on line *1*, the tens place on line *2*. Shifters (PX-4-104) should be used in this terminal to shift the argument if it comes from other decades than the 5th and 6th. The other lines of this terminal are unconnected, so a deleter is not required.

The accumulator which transmits the argument may be programmed from terminals NC and C.

The function table automatically clears its argument at the end of each operation.

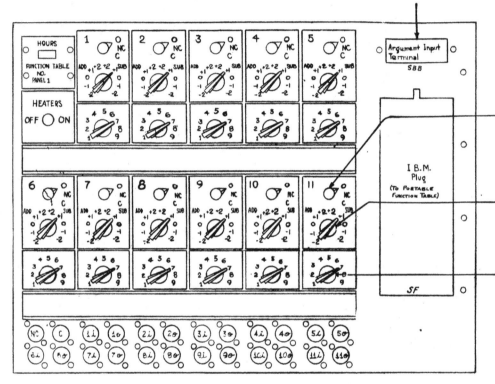

Terminals 11, 21......111
    Program pulse input terminals for program controls 1-11 respectively

Terminals 10, 20......110
    Program pulse output terminals for program controls 1-11 respectively

Terminal NC
    Program pulse output terminal associated with NC on argument reception switch.

Terminal C
    Program pulse output terminal associated with C on argument reception switch.

<u>Time Schedule for Function Table</u>

Addition time	Operation
	(Program input pulse received at end of 0th addition time)
1	Circuits set up
2	Argument received
3	Argument modified by the addition of 0 to 4 pulses. At 14th pulse time portable function table starts to set up.
4	Function table finishes setting up
5	Value of function transmitted
$r+4$	This is continued up to the $r+4$th addition time, where r is the setting of the function repeat switch.
	(Program output emitted at end of $r+4$th addition time)

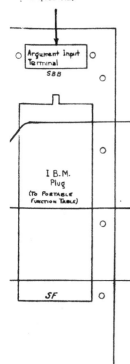

Argument Input
Terminal

SBB

I.B.M.
Plug

(To Portable
Function Table)

SF

There are eleven program controls on each function table. Each program control consists of a program pulse input terminal (which, when stimulated with a program pulse, causes the program control to program the looking up of a function value), a program pulse output terminal (which emits a pulse on completion of the operation), the three switches described below, and an associated transceiver (for neon bulbs see PX-7-305).

Argument reception switch

This switch operates in conjunction with program pulse output terminals NC and C and may be used to program an accumulator or accumulators to transmit the argument.

At the end of the 1st addition time a program pulse is emitted from NC or C if this switch is set on NC or C respectively. Semi-permanent connections may be established by connecting NC and C to program input terminals of the argument accumulator and setting the corresponding operation switches to transmit and transmit-and-clear respectively.

Operation switch

This switch determines whether the function value (add) or its complement (subtract) is transmitted.

It also determines whether the function value of the argument received, or the function value of one of the neighboring arguments, is transmitted. Thus positions-2, -1, 0, +1, +2 give $f(a-2)$, $f(a-1)$, $f(a)$, $f(a+1)$, $f(a+2)$ respectively, where a is the argument.

Operation repeat switch

This switch determines the number of times the function value is transmitted.

Note that 4 addition times are required for the function table to set up, receive the argument, etc. This loss of time must be taken account of in programming the accumulator which receives the value of the function. Thus if that accumulator is programmed with the same pulse that programs the function table with its repeat switch set to 9, it could receive the value of the function only 5 times.

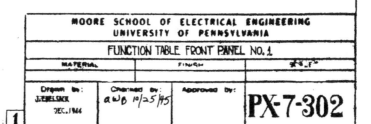

MOORE SCHOOL OF ELECTRICAL ENGINEERING UNIVERSITY OF PENNSYLVANIA			
FUNCTION TABLE FRONT PANEL NO. 1			
MATERIAL	FINISH	SCALE	
Drawn by: J. EBELSICK DEC. 1944	Checked by: a w B 10/25/45	Approved by:	PX-7-302

1

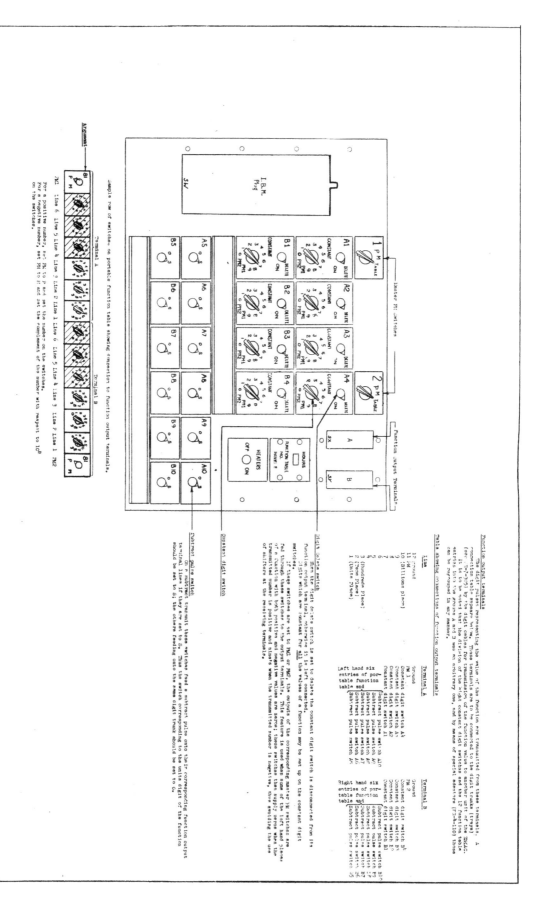

Function output terminals

The digit pulses representing the value of the function are transmitted from these terminals. A connection table appears below. These terminals are to be connected to the connection table entry desired (see PX-7-305) by the digit combination of the function value to number unit of the IBM. It is to be noted that the division of the right constant digit switches and the 12 function table entries into the groups A and B was an arbitrary one, and by means of special adapters (PX-6-110) those can be regrouped in any manner.

Table showing connections of function output terminals

Line	Terminal A	Terminal B
12 ground	Ground	Ground
11 PM 1	PM 1	PM 2
10 (Billions place)	Constant digit switch A4	Constant digit switch B4
9	Constant digit switch A3	Constant digit switch B3
8	Constant digit switch A2	Constant digit switch B2
7	Constant digit switch A1	Constant digit switch B1
6	Constant digit switch A10	Constant digit switch B10
5	Subtract pulse switch A9	Subtract pulse switch B9
4	Subtract pulse switch A8	Subtract pulse switch B8
3 (Hundreds Place)	Subtract pulse switch A7	Subtract pulse switch B7
2 (Tens Place)	Subtract pulse switch A6	Subtract pulse switch B6
1 (Units Place)	Subtract pulse switch A5	Subtract pulse switch B5

Left hand six entries of portable function table end

Right hand six entries of portable function table end

Digit delete switch

When the digit delete switch is set to delete the constant digit switch or function output terminal, otherwise it is left connected. Digits which are constant for all the values of a function may be set up on the constant digit switches.

If these switches are set to PM2 or PM2, the outputs of the corresponding master SW switches are fed through these switches to the output terminal. This feature is used when the sums of the left hand places of a function with both positive and negative values are transmitted number is positive and minus when the transmitted number is negative, thus avoiding the use of shifters at the receiving terminal.

Constant digit switch

Subtract pulse switch

On a subtract pulse, transmit these switches feed a subtract pulse onto their corresponding function output terminal if they are set to 5s. Thus the switch corresponding to the units digit of the function should be set to 6s the others feeding onto the same digit trunk should be set to 6s.

Sample row of switches on portable function table showing connection to function output terminals.

Terminal A

Terminal B

PM1 Line 6 Line 5 Line 4 Line 3 Line 2 Line 1 Line 6 Line 5 Line 4 Line 3 Line 2 Line 1 PM2

For a positive number, set PM1 to p and set the number on the switches.
For a negative number, set PM1 to n and set the complement of the number with respect to 10^6 on the switches.

MOORE SCHOOL OF ELECTRICAL ENGINEERING
UNIVERSITY OF PENNSYLVANIA
FUNCTION TABLE FRONT PANEL NO. 2

Drawn by: J.EMILER DEC.1944
Checked by:
Approved by:

MATERIAL
FINISH
SCALE

PX-7-303

1

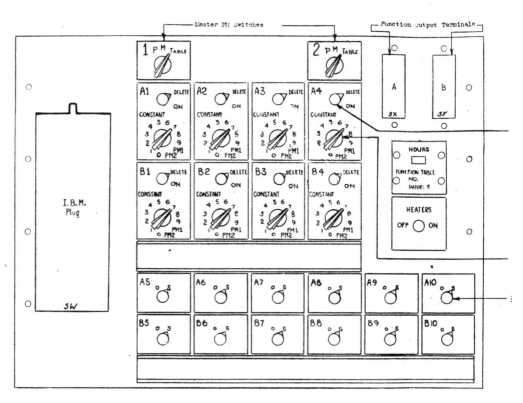

Master FT Switches — Function Output Terminals

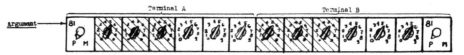

Sample row of switches on portable function table showing connection to function output terminals.

Terminal A   Terminal B

PM1 Line 6 Line 5 Line 4 Line 3 Line 2 Line 1 Line 6 Line 5 Line 4 Line 3 Line 2 Line 1 PM2

For a positive number, set PM to P and set the number on the switches.
For a negative number, set PM to M and set the complement of the number with respect to 10^n on the switches.

Function output terminals

The digit pulses representing the value of the function are transmitted from these terminals. A connection table appears below. These terminals are to be connected to the digit trunks (trays) (see X-7-305) by the digit cables for transmission of the function value to another unit of the ENIAC.

It is to be noted that the division of the eight constant digit switches and the 12 function table entries into the groups A and B was an arbitrary one, and by means of special adaptors (PX-4-110) these can be regrouped in any manner.

Table showing connections of function output terminals

Line	Terminal A	Terminal B
12 ground	Ground	Ground
11 PM	PM 1	PM 2
10 (Billions place)	Constant digit switch A4	Constant digit switch B4
9	Constant digit switch A3	Constant digit switch B3
8	Constant digit switch A2	Constant digit switch B2
7	Constant digit switch A1	Constant digit switch B1
6	Subtract pulse switch A10	Subtract pulse switch B10
5	Subtract pulse switch A9	Subtract pulse switch B9
4	Subtract pulse switch A8	Subtract pulse switch B8
3 (Hundreds Place)	Subtract pulse switch A7	Subtract pulse switch B7
2 (Tens Place)	Subtract pulse switch A6	Subtract pulse switch B6
1 (Units Place)	Subtract pulse switch A5	Subtract pulse switch B5

Left hand six entries of part function table and
Right hand six entries of part function table and

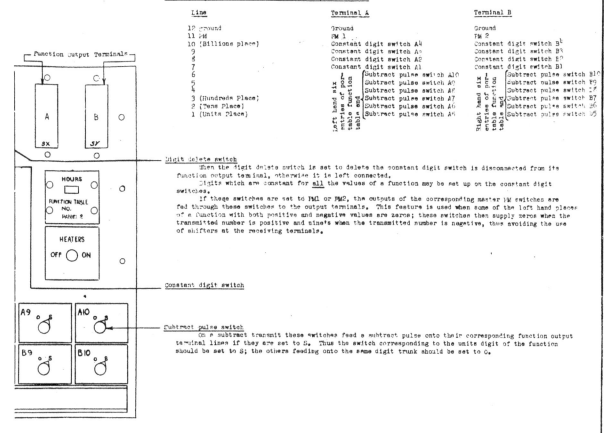

Digit delete switch

When the digit delete switch is set to delete the constant digit switch is disconnected from its function output terminal, otherwise it is left connected.

Digits which are constant for all the values of a function may be set up on the constant digit switches.

If these switches are set to PM1 or PM2, the outputs of the corresponding master PM switches are fed through these switches to the output terminals. This feature is used when some of the left hand places of a function with both positive and negative values are zeros; these switches then supply zeros when the transmitted number is positive and nine's when the transmitted number is negative, thus avoiding the use of shifters at the receiving terminals.

Constant digit switch

Subtract pulse switch

On a subtract transmit these switches feed a subtract pulse onto their corresponding function output terminal lines if they are set to S. Thus the switch corresponding to the units digit of the function should be set to S; the others feeding onto the same digit trunk should be set to O.

on output terminals.

Line 2 Line 1 PM2

respect to 10^D

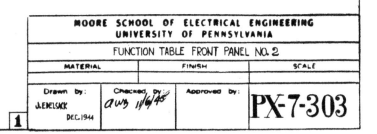

MOORE SCHOOL OF ELECTRICAL ENGINEERING
UNIVERSITY OF PENNSYLVANIA

FUNCTION TABLE FRONT PANEL No. 2

MATERIAL	FINISH	SCALE

Drawn by:	Checked by:	Approved by:	
J. EDELSACK	a w3 11/6/45		PX-7-303
DEC.1944			

1

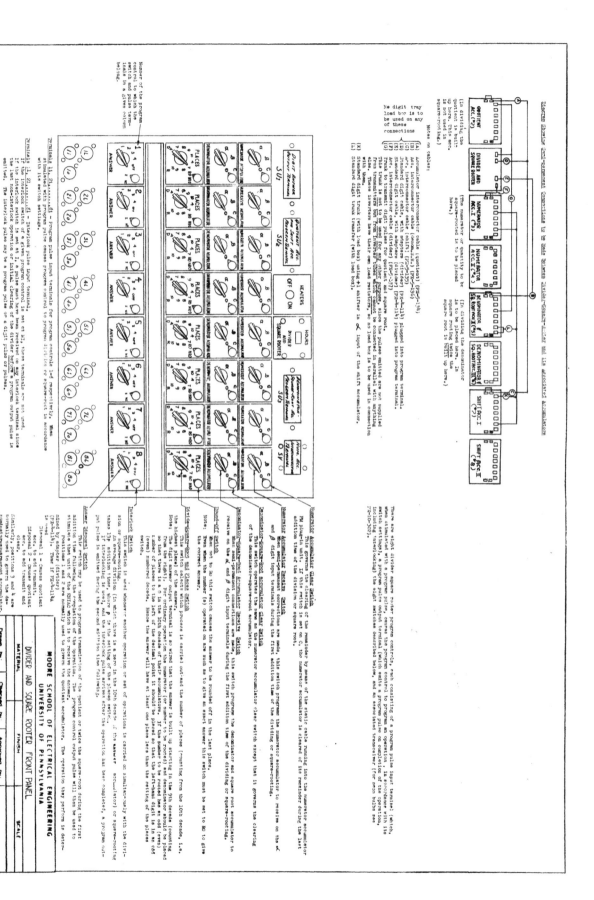

MOORE SCHOOL OF ELECTRICAL ENGINEERING
UNIVERSITY OF PENNSYLVANIA

DIVIDER AND SQUARE ROOTER FRONT PANEL

Drawn by: J.E.DELUKE   DEC.,1914
Checked by: Approved by:
MATERIAL   FINISH   SCALE

PX-10-301

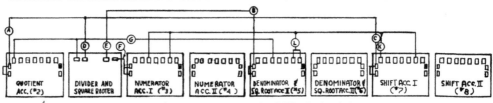

| QUOTIENT ACC. (#2) | DIVIDER AND SQUARE ROOTER | NUMERATOR ACC. I (#3) | NUMERATOR ACC. II (#4) | DENOMINATOR & SQ.ROOT ACC I (#5) | DENOMINATOR & SQ.ROOT ACC.II (#6) | SHIFT ACC. I (#7) | SHIFT ACC. II (#8) |

(In dividing the quotient is built up here. This acc. is not used in square-rooting.)

(The numerator or quantity to be square-rooted is to be placed here.)

(In dividing the denominator is to be placed here. In square rooting twice the square root is built up here.)

No digit tray load box is to be used on any of these connections

Notes on cables:

(A) Accumulator interconnector cable (quotient) (PX-5-134)
(B) Acc. interconnector cable (denom.S.R.) (PX-5-136)
(C) Acc. interconnector cable (shift) (PX-5-135)
(D) Standard digit cable, with adapters (divider) (PX-4-114) plugged into program terminal.
(E) Standard digit cable, with adapters (divider) (PX-4-114) plugged into program terminal.
(F) Acc. interconnector cable (divider) (PX-5-137)
(G) Trunk to transmit digit pulses for quotient and square root. This trunk is not to be used for any other purpose, since the pulses emitted are not supplied from transmitters but from inverter tubes which cannot be connected in parallel with anything else. These inverters have their own load resistors, so no load box is to be used in connection with them.
(K) Standard digit trunk (with load box) using +1 shifter in α input of the shift accumulator.
(L) Standard digit trunk transfer (with load box).

There are
when stimul
switch sett
including
PX-10-302).

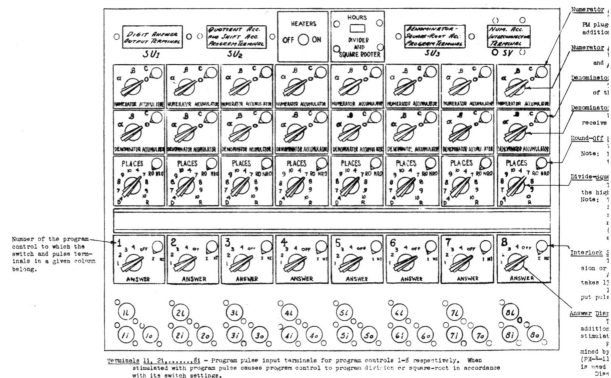

Number of the program control to which the switch and pulse terminals in a given column belong.

Terminals 11, 21,......81 - Program pulse input terminals for program controls 1-8 respectively. When stimulated with program pulse causes program control to program division or square-root in accordance with its switch settings.

Terminals 1i, 2i,......8i - Interlock pulse input terminal,
If the interlock switch of a given program control is set at NI, these terminals are not used.
If the interlock switch is set at I, a pulse must have been received on any interlock terminal since the last non-interlock operation or initial clearing of the divider before a program output pulse is emitted. The interlock pulse may be a program pulse or a digit pulse or pulses.

Terminals 1o, 2o,......8o - Program pulse output terminals for program controls 1-8 respectively. Emits program pulse after both the operation is completed and an interlock pulse is received (if interlock switch is set at I).

Numerator
PM plug
addition

Numerator
and

Denominator
of the

Denominator
receive

Round-Off
Note:

Divide-Squa
the high
Note:

Interlock
sion or
takes 1
put puls

Answer Disp
addition
stimulat
mined by
(PX-4-11
is used
Disp
Disp
Similarl
normally
nominato

SHIFT Acc. II
(V8)

ied
ing
ection

r.

There are eight divider square rooter program controls, each consisting of a program pulse input terminal (which, when stimulated with a program pulse, causes the program control to program an operation, in accordance with its switch settings), a program pulse output terminal (which emits a program pulse on completion of the operation, including interlocking) the eight switches described below, and an associated transceiver (for neon bulbs see PX-10-302).

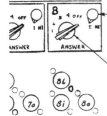

Num. Acc.
Interconnector
Terminal

Numerator Accumulator Clear Switch
This governs the clearing of the remainder by means of the static cable running into the numerator accumulator PM plug-in unit. If this switch is set on C, the numerator accumulator is cleared of its remainder during the last addition time of the division or square root.

Numerator Accumulator Receive Switch
When semi-permanent corrections are made, this switch programs the numerator accumulator to receive on the α and β digit input terminals during the first addition time of the dividing or square-rooting.

Denominator-Square-Root accumulator Clear Switch
This switch operates the same as the numerator accumulator clear switch except that it governs the clearing of the denominator-square-root accumulator.

Denominator-Square-Root Accumulator Receive Switch
When semi-permanent connections are made, this switch programs the denominator and square root accumulator to receive on the α and β digit input terminals during the first addition time of the dividing or square-rooting.

Round-Off Switch
When set to RO this switch causes the answer to be rounded off in the last place.
Note: Even when the number (s) operated on are such as to give an exact answer this switch must be set to RO to give the correct answer.

Divide-Square-Root and Places Switch
This switch selects which process is carried out and the number of places (counting from the 10th decade, i.e. the highest place) of the answer.
Note: The digit answer output terminal is so wired that the answer is built up starting in the 9th decade (counting from the right). For ordinary operation the numerator (or number to be rooted) and denominator should be placed so that there is a 0 in the 10th decade of their accumulators. If the number to be rooted has an odd (even) number of places to the left of the decimal point it should be placed so that the left-hand digit is in an odd (even) numbered decade. Hence the answer will have at least one place less than the setting of the places switch.

Interlock Switch
This switch is used whenever another operation or set of operations is carried on simultaneously with the division or square-rooting.
An average division (in which there is a zero in the 10th decade of the answer accumulator) or square-rooting takes 13p addition times, where p is the setting of the places switch.
If interlocking is used, and the interlock pulse arrives after the operation has been completed, a program output pulse is emitted during the second addition time following.

Answer Disposal Switch
This switch may be used to program transmission of the quotient or twice the square-root during the first addition time following the completion of the operation. The program control output pulse will then be used to stimulate that unit of the ENIAC which is to receive the answer.
Positions 1 and 2 are normally used to govern the quotient accumulator. The operation they perform is determined by adapter (divider)

, When
accordance

sed.
inal since
t pulse is

Emits pro-
terlock

(PX-4-114). Thus if PX-4-114A is used
  Disposal 1 - Causes quotient acc. to add transmit.
  Disposal 2 - Causes quotient acc. to add transmit and clear.
Similarly, positions 3 and 4 are normally used to govern the denominator-square-root accumulator.

MOORE SCHOOL OF ELECTRICAL ENGINEERING UNIVERSITY OF PENNSYLVANIA			
DIVIDER AND SQUARE ROOTER FRONT PANEL			
MATERIAL		FINISH	SCALE
Drawn by: J. EDELSACK DEC. 1944	Checked by: RWS 10/15/45	Approved by:	PX-10-301

No Load Box is used on this tray which carries pulses for the answer. No other units are to be connected into it.

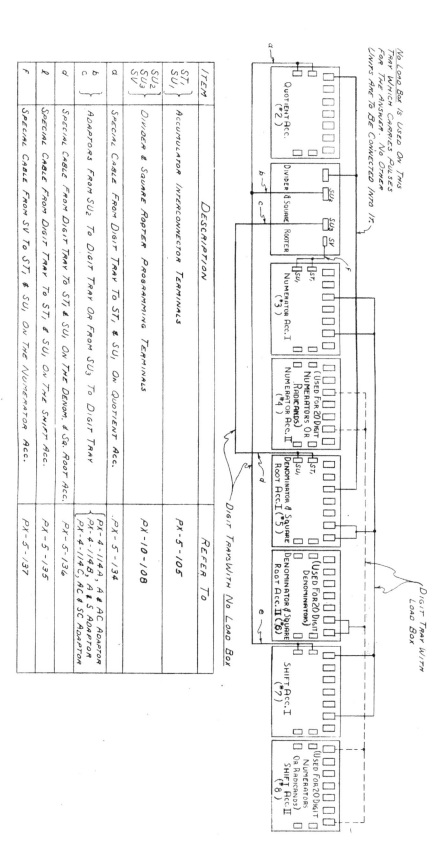

ITEM	DESCRIPTION	REFER TO
ST, SU₁	ACCUMULATOR INTERCONNECTOR TERMINALS	PX-5-105
SU₂, SU₃, SV	DIVIDER & SQUARE ROOTER PROGRAMMING TERMINALS	PX-10-108
a	SPECIAL CABLE FROM DIGIT TRAY TO ST, & SU, ON QUOTIENT ACC.	PX-5-134
b, c	ADAPTORS FROM SU₂ TO DIGIT TRAY OR FROM SU₃ TO DIGIT TRAY	PX-4-114AA, A & AC ADAPTOR / PX-4-114B, A & S ADAPTOR / PX-4-114C, AC & SC ADAPTOR
d	SPECIAL CABLE FROM DIGIT TRAY TO ST, & SU, ON THE DENOM. & SQ. ROOT ACC.	PX-5-136
e	SPECIAL CABLE FROM DIGIT TRAY TO ST, & SU, ON THE SHIFT ACC.	PX-5-135
f	SPECIAL CABLE FROM SV TO ST, & SU, ON THE NUMERATOR ACC.	PX-5-137

QUOTIENT ACC. (#2)

DIVIDER & SQUARE ROOTER

SU₂ SU₃ SV

NUMERATOR ACC. I (#3)

NUMERATOR ACC. II (#4) (USED FOR 20 DIGIT NUMERATORS OR RADICANDS)

DENOMINATOR & SQUARE ROOT ACC. I (#5)

DENOMINATOR & SQUARE ROOT ACC. II (#6) (USED FOR 20 DIGIT DENOMINATORS)

SHIFT ACC. I (#7)

SHIFT ACC. II (#8) (USED FOR 20 DIGIT NUMERATORS OR RADICANDS)

DIGIT TRAY WITH NO LOAD BOX

DIGIT TRAY WITH LOAD BOX

MOORE SCHOOL OF ELECTRICAL ENGINEERING
UNIVERSITY OF PENNSYLVANIA

INTERCONNECTION OF DIVIDER & SQUARE ROOTER WITH
ASSOCIATED ACCUMULATORS ~ PX-10-307

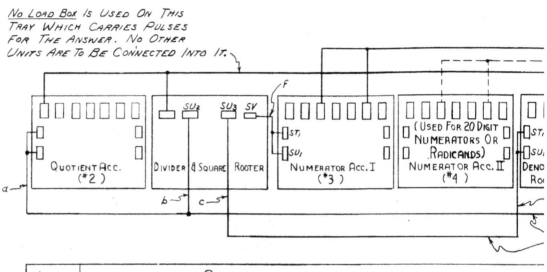

No Load Box Is Used On This Tray Which Carries Pulses For The Answer. No Other Units Are To Be Connected Into It.

ITEM	DESCRIPTION
ST_1 SU_1	ACCUMULATOR INTERCONNECTOR TERMINALS
SU_2 SU_3 SV	DIVIDER & SQUARE ROOTER PROGRAMMING TERMINALS
a	SPECIAL CABLE FROM DIGIT TRAY TO ST_1 & SU_1 ON QUOTIENT ACC.
b c	ADAPTORS FROM SU_2 TO DIGIT TRAY OR FROM SU_3 TO DIGIT TRAY
d	SPECIAL CABLE FROM DIGIT TRAY TO ST_1 & SU_1 ON THE DENOM. & SQ. ROOT
ℓ	SPECIAL CABLE FROM DIGIT TRAY TO ST_1 & SU_1 ON THE SHIFT ACC.
f	SPECIAL CABLE FROM SV TO ST_1 & SU_1 ON THE NUMERATOR ACC.

MOORE SCHOOL OF ELECTRICAL ENGINEERING
UNIVERSITY OF PENNSLVANIA

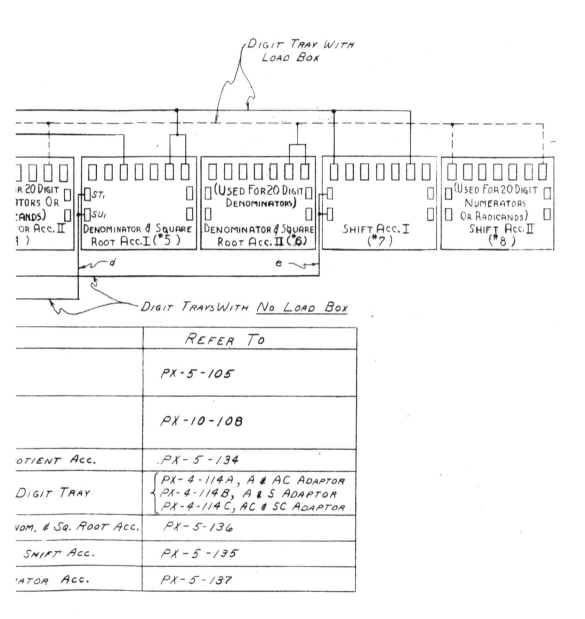

DIGIT TRAY WITH LOAD BOX

(USED FOR 20 DIGIT NUMERATORS OR ...CANDS)

...OR ACC. II (...1)

ST₁
SU₁

DENOMINATOR & SQUARE ROOT ACC. I (#5)

(USED FOR 20 DIGIT DENOMINATORS)

DENOMINATOR & SQUARE ROOT ACC. II (#6)

SHIFT ACC. I (#7)

(USED FOR 20 DIGIT NUMERATORS OR RADICANDS)

SHIFT ACC. II (#8)

d

e

DIGIT TRAYS WITH NO LOAD BOX

	REFER TO
	PX-5-105
	PX-10-108
...OTIENT ACC.	.PX-5-134
...DIGIT TRAY	PX-4-114A, A & AC ADAPTOR PX-4-114B, A & S ADAPTOR PX-4-114C, AC & SC ADAPTOR
...NOM. & SQ. ROOT ACC.	PX-5-136
...SHIFT ACC.	PX-5-135
...ATOR ACC.	PX-5-137

INTERCONNECTION OF DIVIDER & SQUARE ROOTER WITH ASSOCIATED ACCUMULATORS ~ PX-10-307

Digit Output Terminal

Whenever the transmission of a constant is programmed, digit pulses representing this constant are emitted from this terminal. This terminal is to be connected to a digit trunk (tray) (see PX-11-306) by a digit cable for transmission of the constant to another unit of the ENIAC.

A table showing the connecting of this terminal for transmission of the right-hand and right-hand ten digit sets, and combined left- and right-hand five-digit group, is given below. It should be noted that a left-hand five-digit group would be received in the left-hand half of an accumulator and a right-hand five-digit group would be received in the right-hand half if no shifters were used.

*Thus 0 pulses are transmitted on these lines when the constant is positive, 9 pulses when it is a negative, so and 9 pulses when it is a complement. Hence it is unnecessary to use a shifter on a receiving accumulator to receive this constant into the units to ten-thousandths decade of that accumulator.

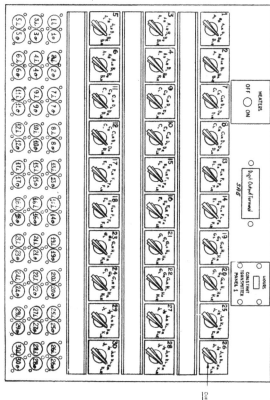

Line	10-digit number (LR)	5-digit left-hand number (L)	5-digit right-hand number (R)
12	Ground	Ground	Ground
11	PM (of L)	PM (of L)	PM (of R)
10	Billions place	Ten-thousandths place	PM (of R)
9			PM (of R)
8			PM (of R)
7		Units place	PM (of R)
6		Tens place	Ten-thousandths place
5	Hundreds place	Hundreds place	
4	Thousandths place	Thousandths place	Tens place
3	Tens place		Hundreds place
2	Tens place	Nothing	Tens place
1	Units place	Nothing	Units place

HEATERS OFF ○ ON ○

○ Digit Output Terminal ○

SAG

○ MOORE ○
CONSTANT
TRANSMITTER
PANEL 1

Constant selector switch

General Explanation of the Constant Transmitter

The constant transmitter has a capacity of 100 digits and 30 signs. These are divided into 10 sets from IBM cards through the IBM reader when proper connections are made on the IBM reader plug board (see PX-11-305). Two of these sets (J,K) are supplied from the constant set switches and PM set switches (see PX-11-905).

Each set may be further divided into two groups, a left-hand group and a right-hand group, each consisting of five digits and a sign. This division must be made in five-digit groups. For example, if the C set is divided into five-digit groups, then any or all of the constant selector switches 7 to 12 may be set to C, or C, but not to C. Conversely, if the C set is not divided, then any or all of constant selector switches 13 to 15 may be set to E, but not to E. The IBM reader controls and plug-board controls are described on PX-11-305.

Constant Transmitter Program Controls

There are 30 constant transmitter program controls, each capable of transmitting certain of the constants over the digit output terminal. Only one program control can be used at a time, hence only one number can be transmitted at a time.

Each program control consists of

1) Program pulse input terminal (when stimulated with program pulse causes program control to transmit the number set on its constant selector switch)
2) Constant selector switch
3) Program pulse input terminal (emits program pulse after constant has been transmitted, i.e., one addition time after the program pulse input terminal has received a pulse.
4) Program controls 1-30 (for neon bulbs see PX-11-306)

Digit Output Terminal

Terminals 1, 2 30
Program pulse output terminals for program controls 1-30

Terminals 1, 2 30
Program pulse input terminals for program controls 1-30

MOORE SCHOOL OF ELECTRICAL ENGINEERING
UNIVERSITY OF PENNSYLVANIA
CONSTANT TRANSMITTER FRONT PANEL NO.1

Drawn By:	Checked By:	Approved By:	
J.EBELMK.			PX-11-302
DEC.1944			

MATERIAL	FINISH	SCALE

1

Digit Output Terminal

Whenever the transmission of a constant is programmed digit pulses representing this constant are emitted from this terminal. This term to a digit trunk (tray) (See PX-11-306) by a digit cable for transmission of the constant to another unit of the ENIAC.

A table showing the connecting of this terminal for left-hand and right-hand five digit groups, and combined left and right-hand ten dig It should be noted that a left-hand five-digit group would be received in the left-hand half of an accumulator and a right-hand five-digit gro the right-hand half if no shifter were used.

Line	10-digit number (LR)	5-digit left-hand number (L)	5-digit r
12	Ground	Ground	Gr
11	PM (of L)	PM (of L)	PM
10	Billions place	Ten-thousandths place	PM
9	. . . .	. . . .	PM
8	. . . .	. . . .	PM
7	. . . .	Tens place*	PM
6	. . . .	Units place	PM
5	. . . .	Nothing	Te
4	. . . .	Nothing	. .
3	Hundreds place	Nothing	. .
2	Tens place	Nothing	Te
1	Units place	Nothing	Un

*Thus 0 pulses are transmitted on these lines when the constant is positive, 9 pulses when it is a complement. Hence it is unnecessary to receiving accumulator to receive this constant into the units to ten-thousands decades of that accumulator.

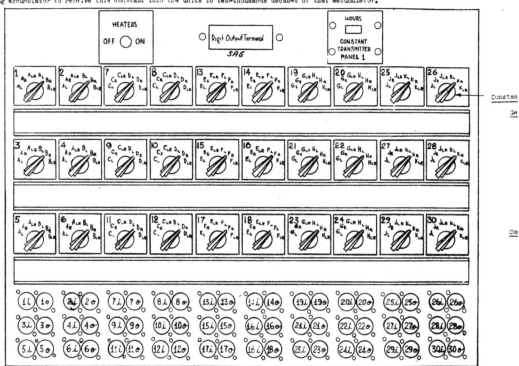

Terminals 1i, 2i 30i
   Program pulse input terminals for program controls 1-30

Terminals 1 , 2 ......,30
   Program pulse output terminals for program controls 1-30

rom this terminal. This terminal is to be connected
ENIAC.
d left and right-hand ten digit sets, appears below.
d a right-hand five-digit group would be received in

bor (L)   5-digit right-hand number (R)

                       Ground
                       PM (of R)
place   PM* (of R)
. . .   PM* (of R)
. . .   PM* (of R)
                       PM (of R)
                       PM* (of R)
                       Ten-thousandths place
                       . . . . .
                       . . . . .
                       Tens place
                       Units place

t. Hence it is unnecessary to use a shifter on a

Constant selector switch

General Explanation of the Constant Transmitter

The constant transmitter has a capacity of 100 digits and 20 signs. These are divided into 10 sets (A,B,....G, J,K,) each consisting of 10 digits and 2 signs. Eight of these sets (A,B,....G) are supplied from IBM cards through the IBM reader when proper connections are made on the IBM reader plug board (see PX-11-305). Two of these sets (J,K) are supplied from the constant set switches and PM set switches of panel 2 (see PX-11-303).

Each set may be further divided into two groups, a left-hand group and a right-hand group, each consisting of 5 digits and a sign. This division must remain fixed throughout a given set-up. For example, if the C set is divided into five-digit groups, then any or all of the constant selector switches 7 to 12 may be set to C_L or C_R but not to C_{LR}. Conversely, if the E set is not divided, then any or all of the constant selector switches 13 to 18 may be set to E_{LR} but not to E_L or E_R.

The IBM reader is programmed from the initiating unit (see PX-9-302). The IBM reader controls and plug-board are described on PX-11-305.

Constant Transmitter Program Controls

There are 30 constant transmitter program controls, each capable of transmitting certain of the constants over the digit output terminal. Only one program control can be used at a time, hence only one number can be transmitted at a time.

Each program control consists of
1) Program pulse input terminal (when stimulated with program pulse causes program control to program transmission of number set on its constant selector switch)
2) Constant selector switch
3) Program pulse output terminal (emits program pulse after constant has been transmitted, i.e., one addition time after the program pulse input terminal has received a pulse.
4) Associated transceiver (for neon bulbs see PX-11-306)

Program controls 1-24, which transmit constants read from the IBM cards, cannot be used during the operation of the card reader, except during the first 50 addition times of this operation. That is, after a pulse is supplied to Ri on the initiating unit front panel (see PX-9-302), these controls may be used during the 50 subsequent addition times, but not thereafter until a pulse is emitted from Ro.

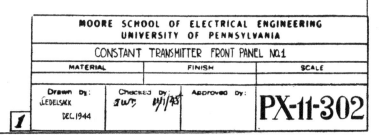

| MOORE SCHOOL OF ELECTRICAL ENGINEERING |
| UNIVERSITY OF PENNSYLVANIA |

| CONSTANT TRANSMITTER FRONT PANEL No.1 |

MATERIAL	FINISH	SCALE

| Drawn by: JEDELSACK DEC.1944 | Checked by: JWT 11/1/45 | Approved by: | PX-11-302 |

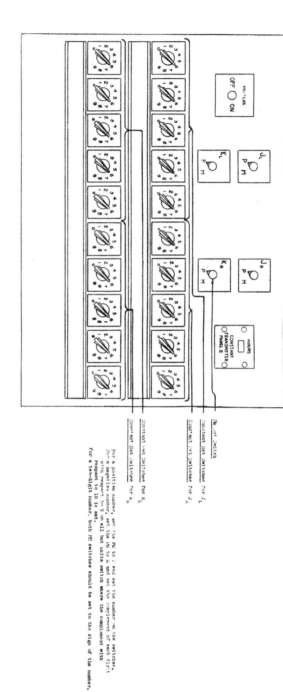

HG.'LES
OFF ○ ON

J_L
P M
○

K_L
P M
○

J_R
P M
○

K_R
P M
○

CONSTANT
TRANSMITTER
PANEL 2
○   ○
HOURS
○   ○

PM Set Switch

Constant Set Switches for J_L

Constant Set Switches for J_R

Constant Set Switches for K_L

Constant Set Switches for K_R

For a positive number, set the PM to + and set the number on the switches.
For a negative number, set the PM to – and set the complement of each digit with respect to 9 on all units switch where the complement with respect to 10 is set.
For a two-digit number, both PM switches should be set to the sign of the number.

MOORE SCHOOL OF ELECTRICAL ENGINEERING
UNIVERSITY OF PENNSYLVANIA

CONSTANT TRANSMITTER FRONT PANEL NO. 2

MATERIAL   FINISH

Drawn by: Checked by: Approved by:
J.LEBELSKIR
DEC.,1944

SCALE

PX-11-303

1

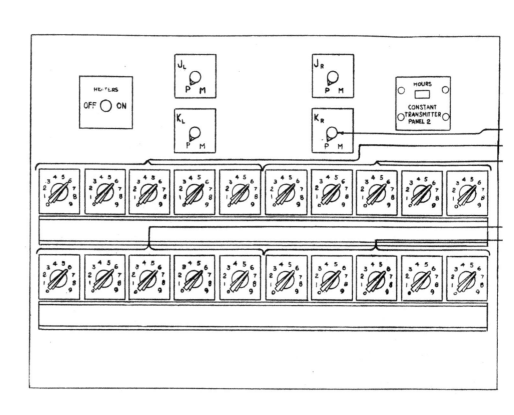

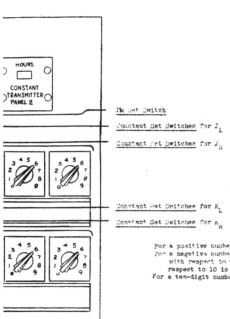

PM Set Switch

Constant Set Switches for J_L

Constant Set Switches for J_R

Constant Set Switches for K_L

Constant Set Switches for K_R

For a positive number, set the PM to J and set the number on the switches.
For a negative number, set the PM to M and set the complement of each digit
    with respect to 9 on all but units switch where the complement with
    respect to 10 is set.
For a ten-digit number, both PM switches should be set to the sign of the number.

MOORE SCHOOL OF ELECTRICAL ENGINEERING
UNIVERSITY OF PENNSYLVANIA

CONSTANT TRANSMITTER FRONT PANEL NO. 2

MATERIAL	FINISH	SCALE

Drawn by:	Checked by:	Approved by:	PX-11-303
J. EDELSACK			
DEC. 1944			

1

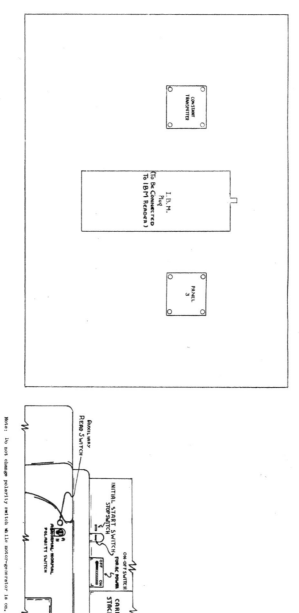

Note: Do not change polarity switch while motor-generator is on.

CONSTANT
TRANSMITTER

I.B.M.
Plug
(To Be Connected
To IBM Reader)

PANEL
3

AUXILIARY
READ SWITCH

INITIAL START SWITCH
STOP SWITCH

ADDITIONAL NORMAL
REVERSAL NORMAL
POLARITY SWITCH

ON OFF SWITCH
FOR AC POWER

OFF
ON

CARD
STACKER

PLUG
BOARD

GREEN
LIGHT

CARD
STACKER
SWITCH

Drawn by
J.L.RELSACK
DEC. 1944

MATERIAL

MOORE SCHOOL OF ELECTRICAL ENGINEERING
UNIVERSITY OF PENNSYLVANIA

CONSTANT TRANSMITTER FRONT PANEL NO.3

Checked by:

FINISH

Approved by:

PX-11-304

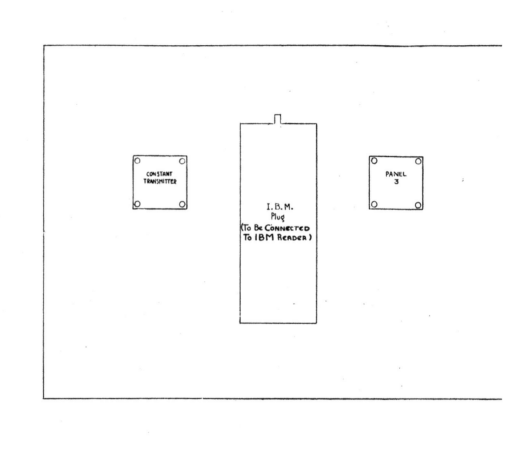

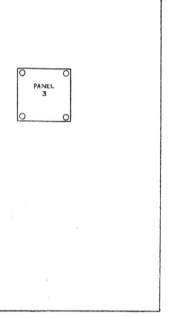

PANEL
3

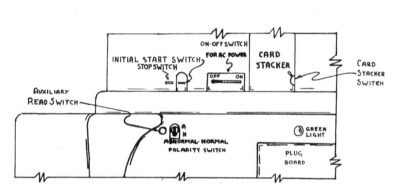

INITIAL START SWITCH
STOP SWITCH

ON-OFF SWITCH
FOR AC POWER

OFF   ON

CARD
STACKER

CARD
STACKER
SWITCH

AUXILIARY
READ SWITCH

A
N
ABNORMAL-NORMAL
POLARITY SWITCH

GREEN
LIGHT

PLUG
BOARD

Note: Do not change polarity switch while motor-generator is on.

MOORE SCHOOL OF ELECTRICAL ENGINEERING
UNIVERSITY OF PENNSYLVANIA

CONSTANT TRANSMITTER FRONT PANEL NO.3

MATERIAL	FINISH	SCALE

Drawn by	Checked by:	Approved by:	
J.E.DELSACK			PX-11-304
DEC.1944			

1

The Polarity Switch

Located on the front of the IBM Reader is a double pole double throw switch which changes the polarity on the holding coils of the relays which control the group selection and the reset control. By plugging this switch one can either wire these circuits in the plug board as described there or in the reverse manner.

(a) With the polarity switch in normal position.
The common terminal "C" is then wired to some hub of the #1 reading brushes and the group selection hubs are wired to hubs of the digit selector. Thus, all controlling is done by various punches in one column. The variety of things controlled is then by plugging to different digits, all being controlled by a punch in some column, say 2, getting an "or" control. That is, if a certain number (12, 11, 0,....,9) is punched in column 21 or column 2 then whatever hub under group selection was plugged to that number of the digit selector causes the corresponding group selection relays to operate.

(b) With the polarity switch in abnormal position.
In this case "C" is wired to some digit on the digit selector and the group selection hubs are wired to various columns. Here, all the control is obtained by a certain punch (for example, a 12 punch) with different things being controlled by plugging to different columns.

Plugging Illustrations

(a) This shows the common hub "C" wired to column 21. The two hubs above and below C are connected so the wire would have gone to either of them. Note that besides the wire (a) one could connect this upper hub for C to some other column, say 2, getting an "or" control. That is, if a certain number (12, 11, 0,...,9) is punched in column 21 or column 2 then whatever hub under group selection was plugged to that number of the digit selector causes the corresponding group selection relays to operate.

(b) This wire causes the reset control to operate whenever there is a 12 punch in column 21; that is, a card with such a punch is called a master card.

(c, d) These leads cause information in storage relay groups 6 and 7 to be held as long as cards come through without a 12 punch in column 21. Whenever a card with a 12 punch in column 21 (a master card) comes along, the information in groups 6 and 7 will be dropped and new information will be put in from this master card. Immediately, the reader will go on to read the next card.

(e) If a card has a 6 punched in column 21 this lead causes group selection relays for group 12 to be activated giving a circuit from C through B instead of A.

(f, g) If a "9" is punched in column 21 groups 15 and 16 group selection relays will be activated. Diagonal leads head (e) and (f) enable one to operate as many groups as desired from just one punch.

(h, i) If there is a 6 punch in column 21 the digit from column 20 will go to the fifth digit of group 6. Otherwise, the digit from column 40 will go there.

(j, k) If there is a 9 punch in column 21 the digit in column 80 will be the fifth digit of group 12. Otherwise, it will be the fifth digit of group 16.

NOTE: If during the course of a computation the IBM reader should run out of cards the starting relay (see PX-11-307) will be closed so the moment new cards are dropped in, the reader will go through a cycle. To make sure that the reader does not fail to feed this first card the stop button should be held down until the cards are firmly in place.

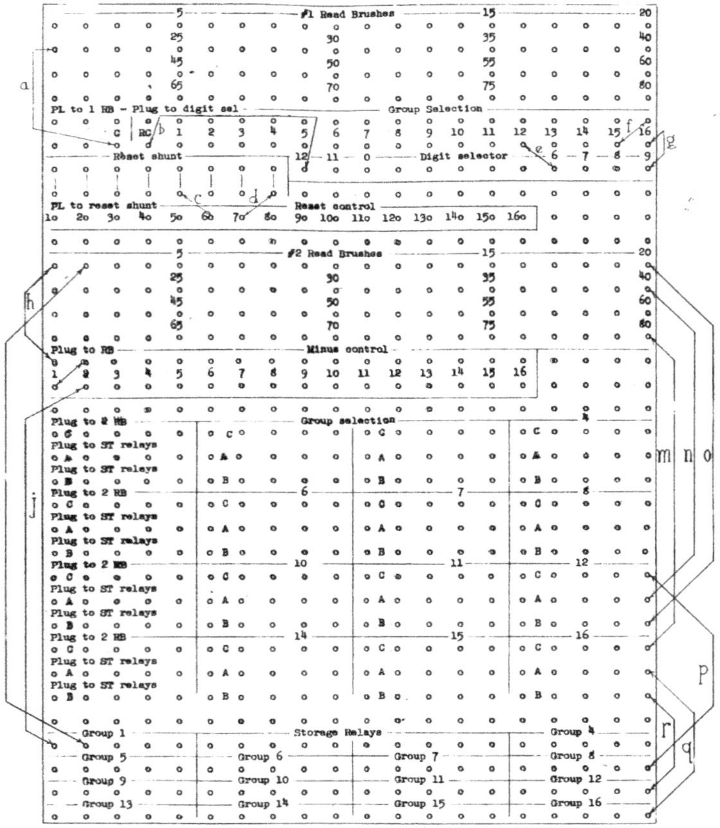

#1 Read Brushes

The #1 Read Brushes read the card before the #2 Read Brushes do. The #1 brushes are double hubs, that is, each hub above and below the number are common. The #1 brushes are used for control purposes and the #2 brushes for reading the numbers and their PW's.

Group Selection

The hubs numbered from one to sixteen control the group selection relays whose terminals are located on the lower half of the plug board. These are double hubs, that is, each hub above and below the number are common. The hubs numbered to the left of these and labeled RG are connected to the same group selection and reset control are described below. For details see the IBM reader wiring diagram PX-11-119.

Reset Control and Reset Shunt

Certain details of relays (depending upon plug board arrangement) are needed to hold information. A particular card is inserted in the sequence of cards. To change the information which is being held in these relays a "master" card is read in these relay until new information is stored in these relays along. Whenever such a master card is read the Reader will immediately read the next detail card before it gives out a computing signal to the ENIAC.

WARNING: The detail cards either must not contain information or else group selection must be plugged to prevent such information from disturbing the held relays.

Group Selection Relays

There are sixteen in the Reader; these terminals connect to the group selection relays. The common terminals are labeled "C" and normally the circuit is through the terminals labeled "A". When the circuit is through the terminals labeled "B", then whatever hub under group selection was plugged to that number causes the corresponding group selection relays to operate.

Minus Control

By means of cams in the Reader these terminals connect to the PW relays of the Constant Transmitter only when the IBM card is in positions 11 and 12, that is, when the punches would be under the #2 Read Brushes. The two hubs, above and below the group number, are common. Usually, a punch for minus indication will occur in the same column that a digit punch appears. Thus, the same reading hub will indicate the PW of the number and later as the positions zero to nine pass under the brushes the digit punches. Other cams (called coding cams) energize the numerical circuits. The detail cards either must contain information or else group selection must be plugged to prevent such information from disturbing the held relays.

Storage Relays

The storage relays are located in the Constant Transmitter and each is associated with each digit. That is, there are essentially four relays representing respectively 1, 2, 2', and 4 in various combinations represent any digit from zero to nine. Thus any number may be set up on the storage relays. The digit punch in that column indicates the numerical circuits to be set up in that Constant Transmitter. The coding cams consist of two groups, one group is used for positive numbers (with respect to the numerical circuits to be set up) and the other group causes complements (with respect to nine) to be set up by storage relays. These complements are used.

For positive numbers the hubs of the storage relays in any column are wired directly to the hubs of the #2 reading brushes which are multiple drives, to indicate the positive number these will be an 11 or 12 punch in some column. The wire from the hub representing this column must go to the minus control hub of all the storage relays used for this negative number. There must also be a connection to the minus responding to this digit in the storage relay used. See the same plugging shown to the left.

Drawn By: J. Cummines, Aug 4, 1945
Checked By / Approved By
12-7-45

MOORE SCHOOL OF ELECTRICAL ENGINEERING
UNIVERSITY OF PENNSYLVANIA

IBM READER PLUG BOARD

MATERIAL / FINISH / SCALE

PX-11-305

The Polarity Switch

Located on the front of the IBM Reader is a double pole double throw switch which changes the polarity on the holding coils of the relays which control the group selection and the reset control. By changing this switch one can either wire these circuits on the plug board in the manner indicated there or in the reverse manner. This gives the following types of control:

(A) With the polarity switch in normal position.
The common terminal "C" is then wired to some hub of the #1 reading brushes and the group selection hubs are wired to hubs of the digit selector. Thus, all controlling is done by various punches in one column. The variety of things controled is given by plugging to different digits (12, 11, 0,.......,9) of the digit selector.

(B) With the polarity switch in abnormal position.
In this case "C" is wired to some digit on the digit selector and the group selection hubs are wired to various columns. Here, all the control is obtained by a certain punch (for example, a 12 punch) with different things being controlled by plugging to different columns.

Plugging Illustrations

(a) This shows the common hub "C" wired to column 21. The two hubs above and below C are connected so the wire could have gone to either of them. Note that besides the wire (a) one could connect this upper hub for C to some other column, say 2, getting an "or" control. That is, if a certain number (12, 11, 0,....,9) is punched in column 21 or column 2 then whatever hub under group selection was plugged to that number of the digit selector causes the corresponding group selection relays to operate.

(b) This wire causes the reset control to operate whenever there is a 12 punch in column 21; that is, a card with such a punch is called a master card.

(c and d) These leads cause information in storage relay groups 6 and 7 to be held as long as cards come through without a 12 punch in column 21. Whenever a card with a 12 punch in column 21 (a master card) comes along the information in groups 6 and 7 will be dropped and new information will be put in from this master card. Immediately, the reader will go on to read the next card.

(e) If a card has a 6 punched in column 21 this lead causes group selection relays for group 12 to be activated giving a circuit from C through B instead of A.

(f and g) If a 9 is punched in column 21 groups 15 and 16 group selection relays will be activated. Diagonal leads such as (f) enable one to operate as many groups as desired from just one punch.

(h, j, and K) This shows the plugging to handle ten digit negative numbers. The PM punch is in column 1 and, by the diagonal connection in the minus control, the PM relays for groups 1 and 2 are operated by this one punch. The first digit reaches the storage relays through (j). (k) illustrates the plugging for the rest of the digits.

(n, o, and p) If there is a 6 punch in column 21 the digit from column 20 will go to the fifth digit of group 8. Otherwise, the digit from column 40 will go there.

(m, q, and r) If there is a 9 punch in column 21 the digit in column 50 will be the fifth digit of group 12. Otherwise, it will be the fifth digit of group 16.

NOTE: If during the course of a computation the IBM reader should run out of cards the starting relay (see PX-11-307) will be closed so the moment new cards are dropped in, the reader will go through a cycle. To make sure that the reader does not fail to feed this first card the stop button should be held down until the cards are firmly in place.

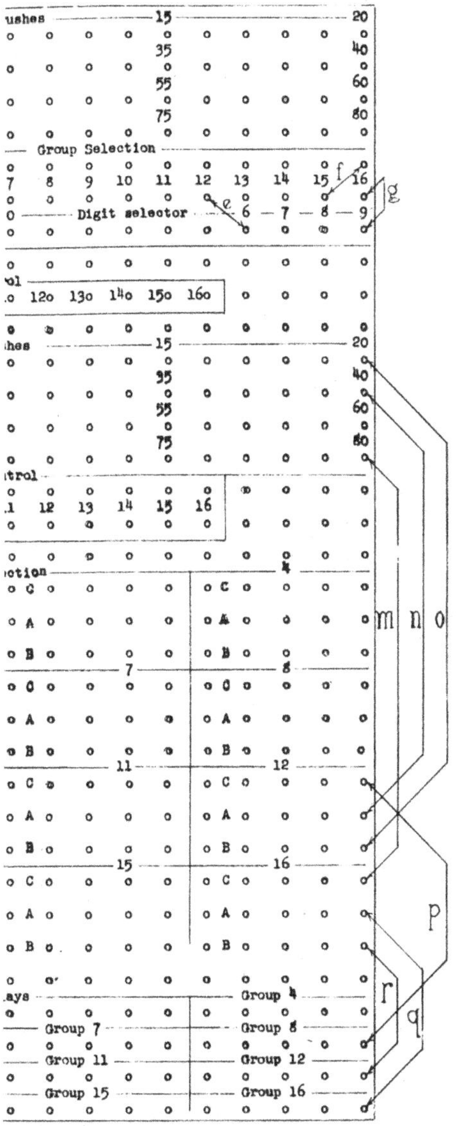

#1 Read Brushes

The #1 Read Brushes read the card before the #2 Read Brushes do. The #1 brushes are used for control purposes and the #2 brushes for reading the numbers and their PM's.

Group Selection

The hubs numbered from one to sixteen control the group selection relays whose terminals are located on the lower half of the plug board. These are double hubs, that is, the hub above and below the number are common. The single hub located to the left of these and labeled RC controls the reset control. The features of group selection and reset control are described below. For details see the IBM reader wiring diagram PX-11-119.

Reset Control and Reset Shunt

Certain groups of relays (depending upon plug board arrangements) may be caused to hold their information while a sequence of "detail" cards are read. This is accomplished by connecting the corresponding terminals under Reset Control to any of the Reset Shunt terminals. To change the information which is being held in these relays a "master" card is inserted in the sequence of cards. A particular punch on this master card can cause the held information to drop out and as the master card passes the #2 Reading Brushes new information can be stored in these relays until the next master card comes along. Whenever such a master card is read the Reader will immediately read the next detail card before it gives out a computing signal to the ENIAC.

WARNING: The detail cards either must not contain information in the fields corresponding to the relays that are holding master card information or else group selection must be used to prevent such information from disturbing the held relays.

Group Selection Relays

There are sixteen five pole double throw relay switches, called the group selection relays. The common terminals are labeled "C" and normally the circuit is through the terminals labeled "A". When activated (picked up) the circuit is through "B". These circuits are isolated (internally) from the other circuits of the reader so there are many other possible plugging arrangements other than those indicated on the plug board.

Minus Control

By means of cams in the Reader these terminals connect to the PM relays of the Constant Transmitter only when the IBM card is in positions 11 and 12, that is, when the PM punches would be under the #2 Read Brushes. The two hubs, above and below the group number, are common. Usually, the punch for minus indication will occur in the same column that a digit punch appears. Thus, the same reading brush will indicate the PM of the number and later as the positions zero to nine pass under the brush indicate the digit punched. Other cams (called coding cams) energize the numerical circuits only during the zero to nine part of the cycle enabling the digit punch in that column to cause the proper relays to be set up in the Constant Transmitter. The coding cams consist of two groups, one group is used for positive numbers and the other group causes complements (with respect to 10^n-1) to be set up by storage relays. The PM relays determine which set of coding cams are used.

Storage Relays

The storage relays are located in the Constant Transmitter. There are essentially four relays associated with each digit. That is, four relays representing respectively 1, 2, 2', and 4 can, in various combinations, represent any digit from zero to nine. These four relays are indirectly (through vacuum tube circuits) associated with the 1, 2, 2', and 4 pulses sent out by the cycling unit. That is, each relay opens a gate tube which through an inverter opens a second gate tube. This second gate tube passes the 1, 2, 2', or 4 pulses.

For positive numbers the hubs of the #2 reading brushes can be wired directly to the hubs of the storage relays in any order whatsoever. Negative numbers must be handled in groups which are multiples of five. To indicate the negative number there will be an 11 or 12 punch in some column. The wire from the hub representing this column must go to the minus control hubs of all the storage relay groups used for this negative number. There must also be a connection to the hub corresponding to this digit in the storage relays. See the examples shown to the left.

MOORE SCHOOL OF ELECTRICAL ENGINEERING
UNIVERSITY OF PENNSYLVANIA

I.B.M. READER PLUG BOARD

MATERIAL	FINISH	SCALE

Drawn by:	Checked by:	Approved by:	
J. Cummings Aug 4, 1945	H. D. Huskey 12-7-45		PX-11-305

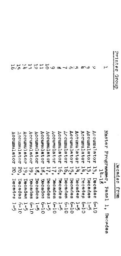

PRINTER
PANEL 1

Coupling Switch

This switch couples two groups of digits together when it is set to to the C position. It provides for the carryover when an ENIAC complement is converted to a true value. The switches of this drawing and PX-12-303 are set for the arrangement shown in the table below.

Table Showing Original Set of Decades Connected to the Printer

Printer Group	Decades from
1	Master Programmer, Panel 1, Decades 14-18
2	Accumulator 13, Decades 6-10
3	Accumulator 13, Decades 1-5
4	Accumulator 14, Decades 6-10
5	Accumulator 14, Decades 1-5
6	Accumulator 15, Decades 6-10
7	Accumulator 15, Decades 1-5
8	Accumulator 16, Decades 6-10
9	Accumulator 16, Decades 1-5
10	Accumulator 17, Decades 6-10
11	Accumulator 17, Decades 1-5
12	Accumulator 18, Decades 6-10
13	Accumulator 18, Decades 1-5
14	Accumulator 19, Decades 6-10
15	Accumulator 19, Decades 1-5
14	Accumulator 20, Decades 6-10
15	Accumulator 20, Decades 1-5
16	Accumulator 20, Decades 1-5

Drawn by: J.F. DRUSHEL DEC. 1944
Checked by: Approved by:
MATERIAL:
MOORE SCHOOL OF ELECTRICAL ENGINEERING
UNIVERSITY OF PENNSYLVANIA
PRINTER FRONT PANEL NO.1
PX-12-301

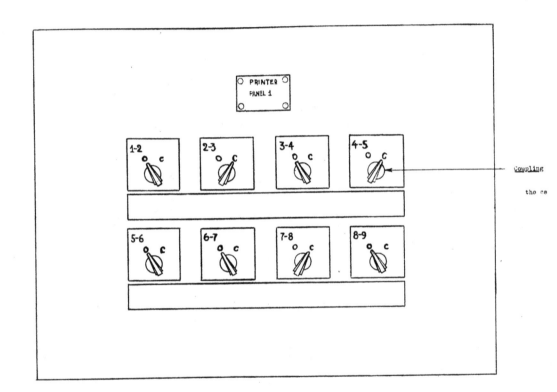

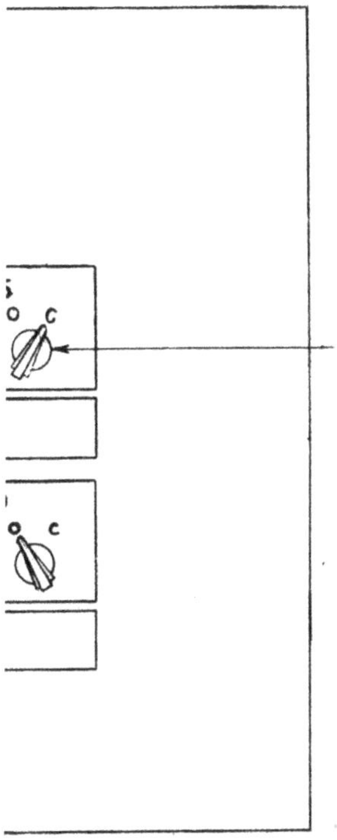

Coupling switch

This switch couples two groups of digits together when it is set to the C position. It provides for the carryover when an ENIAC complement is converted to a true value.

The switches on this drawing and PX-12-303 are set for the arrangement shown in the table below.

Table Showing Original Set of Decades Connected to the Printer

Printer Group	Decades from
1	Master Programmer, Panel 1, Decades 14-18
2	Accumulator 13, Decades 6-10
3	Accumulator 13, Decades 1-5
4	Accumulator 14, Decades 6-10
5	Accumulator 14, Decades 1-5
6	Accumulator 15, Decades 6-10
7	Accumulator 16, Decades 6-10
8	Accumulator 16, Decades 1-5
9	Accumulator 17, Decades 6-10
10	Accumulator 17, Decades 1-5
11	Accumulator 18, Decades 6-10
12	Accumulator 18, Decades 1-5
13	Accumulator 19, Decades 6-10
14	Accumulator 19, Decades 1-5
15	Accumulator 20, Decades 6-10
16	Accumulator 20, Decades 1-5

MOORE SCHOOL OF ELECTRICAL ENGINEERING
UNIVERSITY OF PENNSYLVANIA

PRINTER FRONT PANEL No. 1

MATERIAL   FINISH

Drawn by: Checked by: Approved by:
J. EDELSACK   A.W.B. 10/24/45
DEC. 1944

PX-12-301

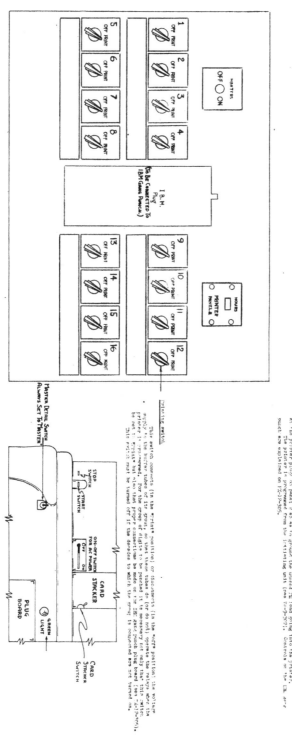

Printer Front Panel No. 2

MASTER
OFF ○ ON

HOURS
PRINTER PANEL

I.B.M. Plug
(To Be Connected to IBM Gang Punch)

1 OFF PRINT	2 OFF PRINT	3 OFF PRINT	4 OFF PRINT
5 OFF PRINT	6 OFF PRINT	7 OFF PRINT	8 OFF PRINT
9 OFF PRINT	10 OFF PRINT	11 OFF PRINT	12 OFF PRINT
13 OFF PRINT	14 OFF PRINT	15 OFF PRINT	16 OFF PRINT

STOP SWITCH
START SWITCH
ON-OFF SWITCH FOR AC POWER   OFF ON
CARD STACKER
PLUG BOARD
GREEN LIGHT
CARD STACKER SWITCH

Master Detail Switch
Always Set to Master

General Explanation of Printer

The printer operates from the static outputs of accumulator and master programmer decades.

Printing switch

This switch connects (in the "print" position) or disconnects (in the "off" position) ...

MOORE SCHOOL OF ELECTRICAL ENGINEERING
UNIVERSITY OF PENNSYLVANIA
PRINTER FRONT PANEL NO. 2

Drawn by: J.L EMELSACK DEC 1944
Checked by:
Approved by:
MATERIAL   FINISH   SCALE

PX-12-302

I

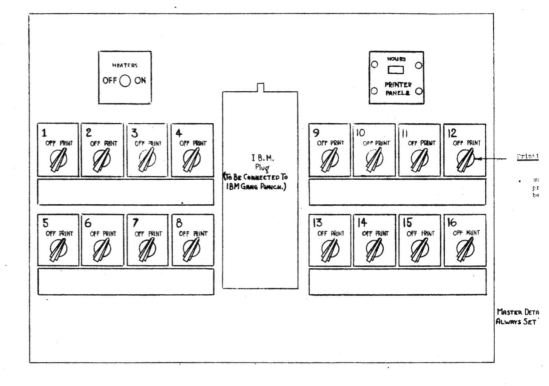

Printi

Master Deta
Always Set

General Explanation of Printer

The printer operates from the static outputs of accumulator and master programmer decades. The cables connecting the decade static terminals to the printer lie in a trough at the top of the front of the machine. A table, showing the original set of connections, appears on PX-12-301. Every accumulator decade and PM unit and every master programmer decade has a static output terminal.

The numbers to be printed are divided into sixteen groups of 5 digits and a PM, numbered from 1 to 16. The printing switches determine which groups are connected to the IBM gang punch. Drawing PX-12-305 shows the IBM gang punch plug board and gives instructions for connecting it up. Any group of five digits and a PM may be connected to an adjacent group by means of the coupling switch, so that 10 digit, 15 digit, etc. numbers may be punched.

When the number to be printed is a complement (i.e., the PM counter registers M), the true value of the number is punched along with an 11 punch to indicate that it is negative.

Whenever information in the master programmer is printed adaptor PX-12-114 B must be used at the printer plugs on panel 2 so as to ground the unused PM lead going into the printer.

The printer is programmed from the initiating unit (see PX-9-302). Controls on the IBM gang punch are explained on PX-12-305.

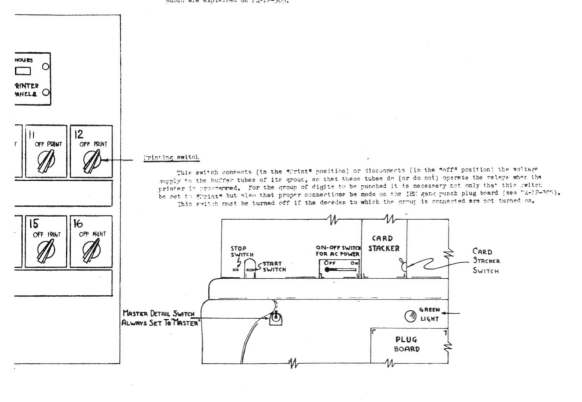

Printing switch

This switch connects (in the "print" position) or disconnects (in the "off" position) the voltage supply to the buffer tubes of its group, so that these tubes do (or do not) operate the relays when the printer is programmed. For the group of digits to be punched it is necessary not only that this switch be set to "print" but also that proper connections be made on the IBM gang punch plug board (see PX-12-305).

This switch must be turned off if the decades to which the group is connected are not turned on.

MOORE SCHOOL OF ELECTRICAL ENGINEERING
UNIVERSITY OF PENNSYLVANIA

PRINTER FRONT PANEL NO. 2

MATERIAL	FINISH	SCALE

| Drawn by: J. EDELSACK DEC. 1944 | Checked by: aws 11/11/45 | Approved by: | PX-12-302 |

1

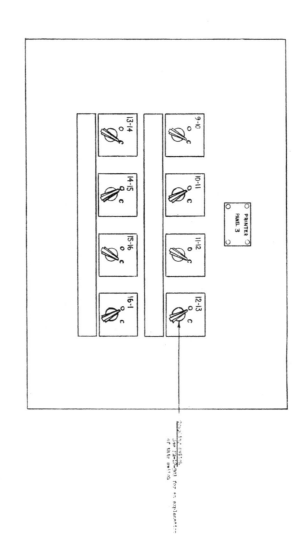

MOORE SCHOOL OF ELECTRICAL ENGINEERING
UNIVERSITY OF PENNSYLVANIA
PRINTER FRONT PANEL NO.3

MATERIAL		
DRAWN BY: J.EDELMER DEC.1944	CHECKED BY:	APPROVED BY:

PX-12-303

PLUG BOARD FOR GANG PUNCH

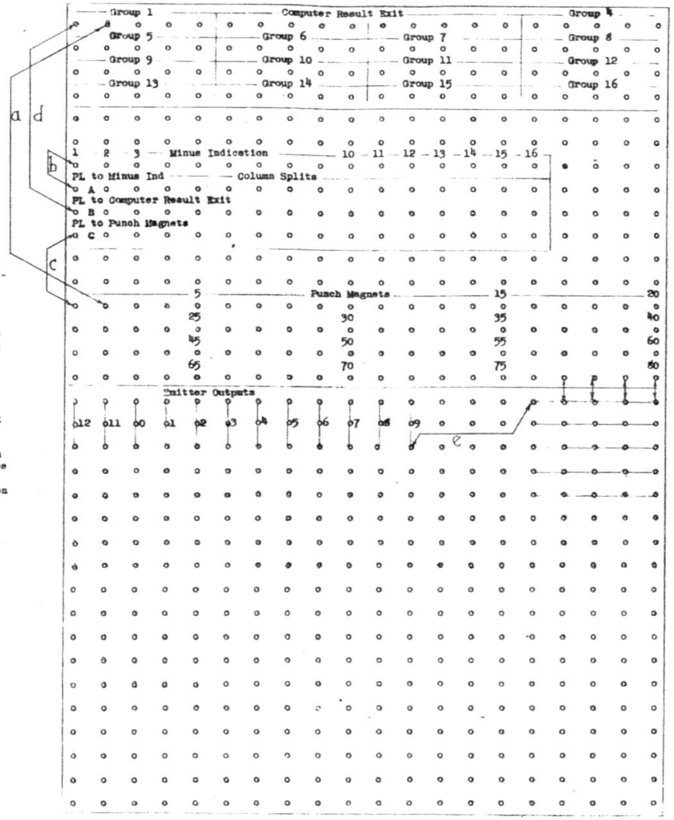

Computer Result Exit

These hubs connect directly to the digit relays in the printer. To punch positive numbers they can be plugged to the punch magnet hubs in any desired arrangement. Thus, it is possible to place the digits coming from the group 1 relays in any five of the eighty columns on the IBM card.

Minus Indication.

The sixteen hubs under minus indication go directly to the PM relays of the sixteen groups. The minus indication of any group could be punched in any of eighty columns on the card simply by connecting the corresponding minus indication hub with the particular column hub of the punch magnet.

Usually, however, the minus indication will appear above some digit of the number on the card. To place the minus indication of the corresponding group in plugged to one of the terminals labeled "A" under column splits, The hubs "B" and "C" directly under the A-hub used are to be plugged, respectively, to the digit hub (Computer Result Exit) above which the minus indication is desired and to the corresponding hub of the punch magnet.

The column splits is simply a sixteen pole double throw relay switch. This switch is controlled by a cam in the IBM punch which causes the "C" hub to be connected to the respective "A" hubs during the ll position of the card and to the "B" hubs during the 0,......9 position of the card.

Emitter Outputs

If one of these hubs is plugged to a punch magnet hub the corresponding number will be punched in that column of the card. The five rows of five common hubs to the right of the emitter outputs enable one to punch the same number in more than three columns. The connection labeled (e) on the diagram causes nines to be punched in columns 77......80 on the card. Connections such as these cause the corresponding number to be punched in every card. This can be used to drive identifying numbers to the cards or to punch dates on the cards. Alphabetic punching cannot be done on this machine.

Plugging Illustrations

(a) This illustration the type of plugging in columns where no minus indication is desired.

(b, c, and d) When the ll position of the card is under the punch magnet there is connection through leads (c) and (d) from the punch magnet hub to the minus indicating, If from the group 1 PM relays were activated a signal will arrive at this time causing the ll to be punched in column 1 on the card. If the ll punch indicating a negative number were desired in column 2 leads (a) and (c) must be interchanged at the punch magnet hubs and leads (b) and (d) interchanged at the computer exit hubs. Then the first column of the computer exit goes directly to the first column punch and the second column leads go through the minus indication hubs and the column split.

(e) These connections will cause nines to be punched in the last four columns on the card.

MOORE SCHOOL OF ELECTRICAL ENGINEERING
UNIVERSITY OF PENNSYLVANIA

MATERIAL: IBM GANG PUNCH PLUG BOARD

Drawn By:
Checked By:
Approved By:

PX12-305

Computer Result Exit

These hubs connect directly to the digit relays in the printer. To punch positive numbers they can be plugged to the punch magnet hubs in any desired arrangement. Thus, it is possible to place the digits coming from the group 1 relays in any five of the eighty columns on the IBM card.

Minus Indication.

The sixteen hubs under minus indication go directly to the PM relays of the sixteen groups. The minus indication of any group could be punched in any of eighty columns on the card simply by connecting the corresponding minus indication hub with the particular column hub of the punch magnets.

Usually, however, the minus indication will appear above some digit of the number on the card. To place the minus indication (an 11 punch) above the first digit of the number the minus indication of the corresponding group is plugged to one of the terminals labeled "A" under column splits. The hubs "B" and "C" directly under the A-hub used are to be plugged, respectively, to the digit hub (Computer Results Exit) above which the minus punch is desired and to the corresponding hub of the punch magnets.

The column splits is simply a sixteen pole double throw relay switch. This switch is controlled by a cam in the IBM punch which causes the "C" hubs to be connected to the respective "A" hubs during the 11 position of the card and to the "B" hubs during the 0,......,9 position of the card.

Emitter Outputs

If one of these hubs is plugged to a punch magnet hub the corresponding number will be punched in that column of the card. The five rows of five common hubs to the right of the emitter outputs enable one to punch the same number in more than three columns. The connection labeled (e) on the diagram causes nines to be punched in the columns 77,....,80 on the card. Connections such as these cause the corresponding number to be punched in every card. This can be used to give identifying numbers to the cards or to punch dates on the cards. Alphabetic punching cannot be done on this machine.

PLUG BOARD FOR GANG PUNCH

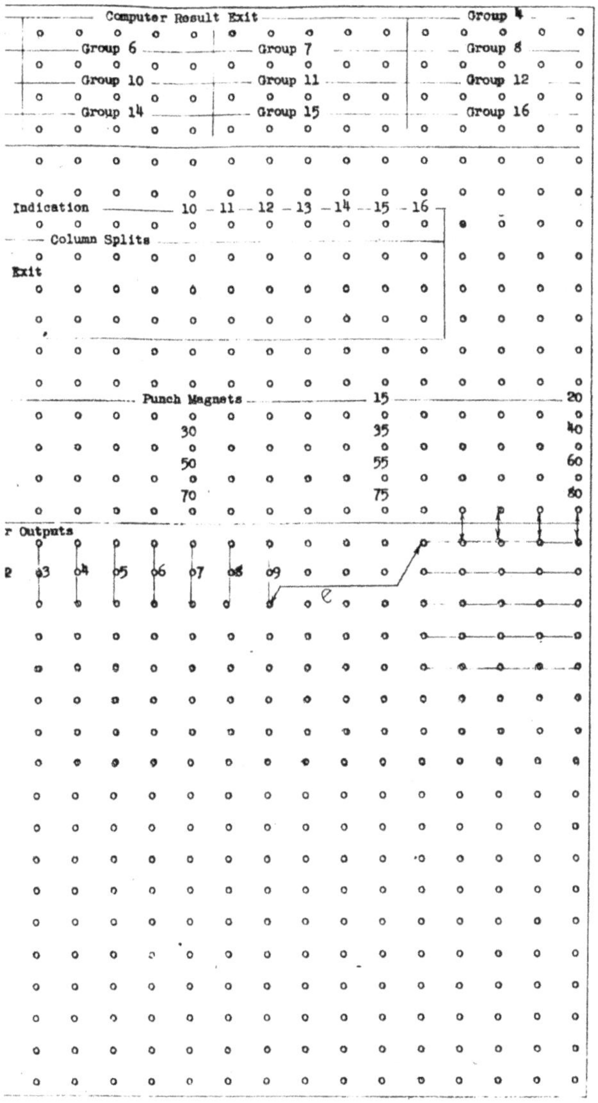

Plugging Illustrations

(a) This illustrates the type of plugging in columns where no minus indication is desired.

(b, c, and d) When the 11 position of the card is under the punches there is a connection through leads (c) and (d) from the punch magnet hub to the minus indication. If the group 1 PM relays were activated a signal will arrive at this time causing the 11 to be punched in column 1 on the card. If the 11 punch indicating a negative number were desired in column 2 leads (a) and (c) must be interchanged at the punch magnet hubs and leads (a) and (d) interchanged at the computer exit hubs. Then the first column of the computer exit comes directly to the first column punch and the second column leads go through the minus indication hubs and the column split.

(e) These connections will cause nines to be punched in the last four columns on the card.

MOORE SCHOOL OF ELECTRICAL ENGINEERING
UNIVERSITY OF PENNSYLVANIA

I.B.M GANG PUNCH PLUG BOARD

MATERIAL	FINISH	SCALE

Drawn by:	Checked by:	Approved by:	
J. Cummings 12. 4. 45	12. 7. 45		PX-12-305

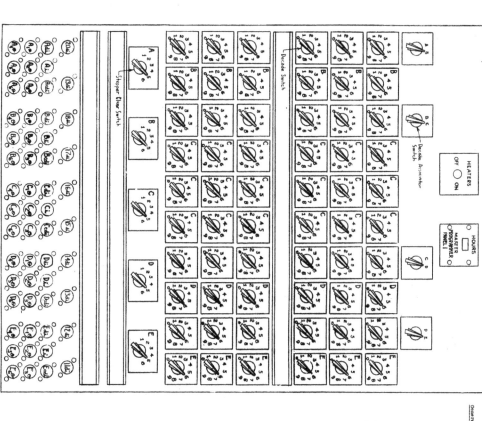

HEATERS OFF ○ ON

HOURS ○ MASTER ○ PROGRAMMER PANEL 1

General Explanation of Steppers and Decades

A stepper is a six stage ring counter. It has the following associated with it:

1) Stepper program pulse input terminal
2) Six stepper program pulse output terminals, one associated with each stage of the stepper.
3) A group or decades (of from 0 to 5, depending upon the stepper and the settings of the associated decade switches. The 6 (=50...5) decades of each group are inter-connected by a direct carry-over circuit [There is no delayed carry-over circuit]
   4) Stepper clear input terminal
   5) Stepper direct input terminal
   6) Stepper clear direct input terminal
   7) Each decade has a direct input terminal.

The operation of a stepper and its associated equipment is as follows...

Decade Switch

Decade Associator

B C   Decade Switch

Stepper Clear Switch

Stepper terminals

A₁o......Kı
A₂o......Kₒ₂....Kₒ   Kₒo......Kₒ₆
A₃l......KDl
A₄ol.....KDl
Decade terminals   D₄l₂o.....D₄ll

Stepper program pulse input terminals
Stepper program pulse output terminals
Stepper clear input terminals
Stepper direct input terminal
Stepper clear direct input terminals

Decade direct input terminals

Program Pulse   **Operation**

0   Input program pulse (to Dı)
1   Output program pulse emitted (from Dₗo,....Dₗo)
2   ...

To disassociate a decade from its stepper pull out gets tube 65 in the stepper plug-in unit.
See block diagram PX-8-30A.

Terminals Al, Bl,............Kl   Stepper program pulse input terminals

Terminals A₂o...........Kₒ
   A₂o...........Kₒ
   A₃o...........Kₒ
   A₄o...........Kₒ   Stepper program pulse output terminals associated with Stage 1
   Stage 2
   Stage 6

Terminals Aₒl,.......Kₒl   Stepper clear input terminal

Terminals A₄ol,.......KDl   Stepper direct input terminals

Drawn By: J.PRESPER   Checked By: Approved By:
DEC.1944
MATERIAL   FINISH   SCALE

MOORE SCHOOL OF ELECTRICAL ENGINEERING
UNIVERSITY OF PENNSYLVANIA
MASTER PROGRAMMER FRONT PANEL NO. 1

PX-8-30A

1

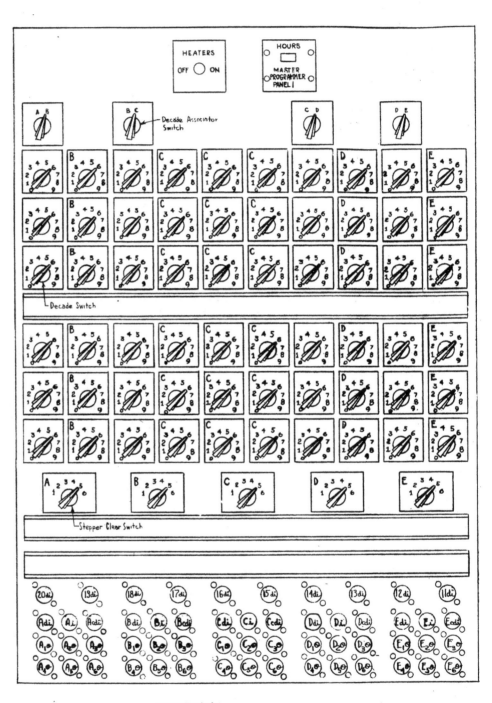

Stepper terminals

$A_1, \ldots \ldots, K_1$	Stepper program pulse input terminals
$A_1 o, \ldots, A_6 o; \ldots K_1 o, \ldots K_6 o$	Stepper program pulse output terminals
$Adi, \ldots, Kdi$	Stepper direct input terminals
$Acdi, \ldots, Kcdi$	Stepper clear direct input terminals

Decade terminals

$Ddi20, \ldots, Ddi1$	Decade direct input terminals

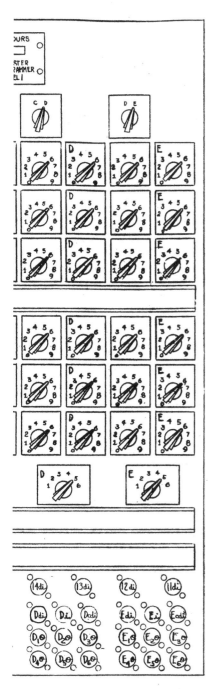

General Explanation of Steppers and Decades

A stepper is a six stage ring counter. It has the following associated with it:

1) Stepper program pulse input terminal
2) Six stepper program pulse output terminals, one associated with each stage of the stepper.
3) A group of decades (of from 0 to 5, depending upon the stepper and the settings of the decade associator switches. The n ($n = 0, \ldots, 5$) decades of each group are interconnected by a direct carry-over circuit (there is no delayed carry-over circuit) enabling them to count (not accumulate) $10^n - 1$ pulses.
4) Stepper clear switch
5) Stepper direct input terminal
6) Stepper clear direct input terminal
7) Each decade has a direct input terminal

The operation of a stepper and its associated equipment is as follows:

At the end of the initial clear each stepper is left on the 1st stage and each decade is cleared to 0.

Suppose a program pulse is received on a stepper program pulse input terminal. One addition time later a program pulse is emitted from the program pulse output terminal corresponding to the stage the stepper is on at the time it is emitted and a program pulse is sent to the units decade of the group of associated decades.

Whenever a group of decades counts to the number set on those decade switches corresponding to the position of the stepper, one addition time later these decades are cleared to zero and the stepper is either stepped to the next position, or (if it is on the position set on its stepper clear switch) cleared to the first position. Though the decades will count either program pulses or digit pulses, any pulse which might cause this clearing and stepping action must be a program pulse.

The decades count both the pulses supplied to the associated stepper's program pulse input terminal (with a one addition time delay) and those supplied to the decade direct input terminals. No set-up is permissible which might lead to pulses being supplied to a decade from both sources simultaneously, or from a decade direct input terminal and a carry-over from a previous decade simultaneously.

An example illustrating a common application of a stepper in programming will show how items 1 through 4 operate together. Consider stepper D, and suppose that decades 12 and 13 are associated with it and that its stepper clear switch is set to 4. Then four two-digit numbers ($n_1, \ldots, n_4$) may be set up on the decade switches, each number associated with the corresponding stage ($1 \ldots 4$) of the stepper and hence with the corresponding program pulse output terminals ($D_{10}, \ldots, D_{40}$). Whenever a program pulse is received on D_1 a pulse is emitted from one of the output terminals (one addition time later). The first n_1 pulses received on D_1 are emitted from D_{10}; the next n_2 pulses received on D_1 are emitted from $D_{20}, \ldots, \ldots$, the last n_4 pulses received on D_1 are emitted from D_{40}, and the stepper and its associated decades are then left in their original state, ready to repeat the process. The time schedule of these operations is as follows:

Program Pulse	Operation
0	Input program pulse (to Di)
1	Output program pulse emitted (from $D_{10}, \ldots D_{40}$)
	Decade stepped to next stage
2	In case the decades register the number set up on the decade switches, all decades (associated with stepper D) are cleared to zero and the stepper (D) is stepped to the next stage or (if it is on the position 4) it is cleared to the first stage.

To disassociate a decade from its stepper pull out gate tube 63 in the stepper plug-in unit. See block diagram PX-8-304.

Terminals Ai, Bi, ...Ki	Stepper program pulse input terminals
Terminals $A_{10}, \ldots \ldots \ldots \ldots K_{10}$	Stepper program pulse output terminals associated with Stage 1
$A_{20}, \ldots \ldots \ldots \ldots K_{20}$	Stage 2, ...
$A_{60}, \ldots \ldots \ldots \ldots K_{60}$	Stage 6

One addition time after a program pulse is supplied to an input terminal (such as Di) a program pulse is emitted from the output terminal corresponding to the stage the stepper is on at the time it is emitted (thus if the stepper is at position 4, when the pulse is emitted it comes from D_{40}), and a unit is added to the contents of the associated decades.

Terminals Acdi, ... Kcdi	Stepper clear direct input terminals.

A pulse supplied to this terminal will clear the stepper to the first position. If a clearing pulse and a stepping pulse arrive at the same time, the stepper will be cleared, not stepped.

MOORE SCHOOL OF ELECTRICAL ENGINEERING
UNIVERSITY OF PENNSYLVANIA

MASTER PROGRAMMER FRONT PANEL NO. 1

MATERIAL	FINISH	SCALE

Drawn by: J. EDELSACK DEC. 1944	Checked by: D. B. 10/18/45	Approved by:	PX-8-301

Stepper program pulse input terminals
Stepper program pulse output terminals
Stepper direct input terminals
Stepper clear direct input terminals

Decade direct input terminals

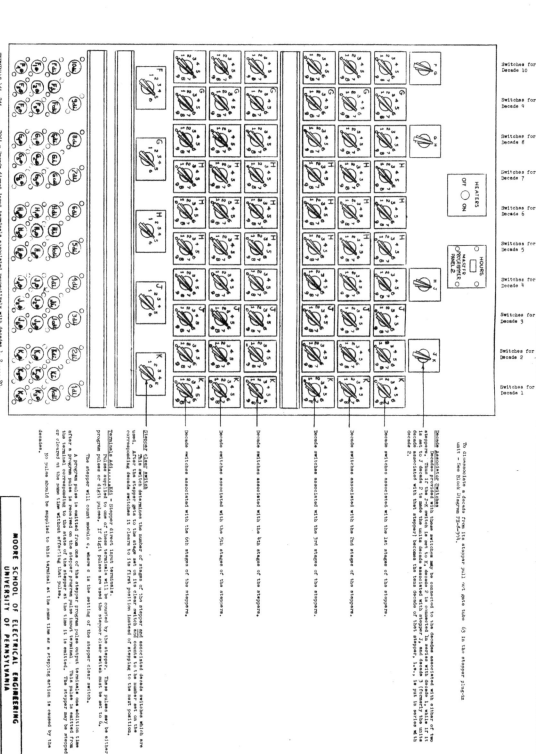

Switches for Decade 10

Switches for Decade 9

Switches for Decade 8

Switches for Decade 7

Switches for Decade 6

Switches for Decade 5

Switches for Decade 4

Switches for Decade 3

Switches for Decade 2

Switches for Decade 1

HEATERS OFF ○ ON

MASTER PROGRAMMER PANEL 2

HOURS

Decade Associator Switches

Decades provided with these switches may be connected to the decades associated with either of two steppers. Thus if the J-K switch is set to K, decade 2 is connected in series with decade 1, while if it is set to J decade 2 is made the units decade associated with stepper J, and decade 3 (formerly the units decade associated with that stepper) becomes the tens decade of that stepper, i.e., is put in series with decade 2.

To dissociate a decade from its stepper pull out gate tube 63 in the stepper plug-in unit - See Block Diagram PX-8-393.

Stepper Clear Switch

This switch determines the number of stages of the stepper and associated decade switches which are used. After the stepper gets to the stage set on its clear switch and counts to the number set on the corresponding decade switches it clears to its first position instead of stepping to the next position.

Decade switches associated with the 6th stages of the stepper.

Decade switches associated with the 5th stages of the stepper.

Decade switches associated with the 4th stages of the stepper.

Decade switches associated with the 3rd stages of the stepper.

Decade switches associated with the 2nd stages of the stepper.

Decade switches associated with the 1st stages of the stepper.

TERMINALS A4↑, B4↑, ...K6↑ - Stepper direct input terminals.

Pulses supplied to one of these terminals will be counted by the stepper. These pulses may be either program pulses or digit pulses. If digit pulses are used the stepper can advance.

The stepper will count modulo c, where c is the setting of the stepper clear switch.

A program pulse is emitted from one of the stepper program pulse output terminals one addition time after a program pulse is received on the stage set on the clear switch and counts to the number set on the decade associated to the state of the stepper at the time it is emitted. This pulse is emitted from or cleared at the same time without affecting that pulse. The stepper may be stepped or cleared at the same time as a stepping action is caused by the decades.

No pulse should be supplied to this terminal at the same time as a stepping action is caused by the decades.

TERMINALS 1d↑, 2d↑, ...20d↑ - Decade direct input terminals associated respectively with decades 1, 2, ..., 20. (counted from right to left)

Pulses supplied to these terminals will be counted by the decades. These pulses may be either program or digit pulses though any pulse which steps the decades to the number set up on the decade switches corresponding to position of the stepper must be a program pulse, and any pulse which causes a carry-over must be a program pulse.

No program pulse should be supplied to the decade direct input of the units decade of a program pulse time following the reception of a program pulse on the decade direct input or that stepper. Pulses can be fed into the direct input terminals of that stepper, i.e. are no carry-over pulses from previous decades of the set. Pulses of decades other than the units decade only at times when there are no carry-over pulses from previous decades of the set.

MOORE SCHOOL OF ELECTRICAL ENGINEERING
UNIVERSITY OF PENNSYLVANIA
MASTER PROGRAMMER FRONT PANEL NO. 2

Drawn by: J.FRELINK	Checked by:	Approved by:
DEC. 1944		PX-8-302
MATERIAL	FINISH	SCALE

TERMINALS 1di, 2di, ...,20di = Decade direct input terminals associated respectively with decades 1, 2,....,20. (counted from right to left)

   Pulses supplied to these terminals will be counted by the decades. These pulses may be either program or digit pulses, though any pulse which steps the decades to the number set up on the decade switches corresponding to position of the stepper must be a program pulse, and any pulse which causes a carry-over must be a program pulse.
   No program pulse should be supplied to the decade direct input of the units decade of a stepper one addition time following the reception of a program pulse on the program pulse input terminal of that stepper.
   Pulses can be fed into the direct input terminals of decades other than the units decade only at times when there are no carry-over pulses from previous decades of the set.

To disassociate a decade from its stepper pull out gate tube 63 in the stepper plug-in unit - See Block Diagram PX-8-304.

Decade Associator Switches

Decades provided with these switches may be connected to the decades associated with either of two steppers. Thus if the J-K switch is set to K, decade 2 is connected in series with decade 1, while if it is set to J decade 2 is made the units decade associated with stepper J, and decade 3 (formerly the units decade associated with that stepper) becomes the tens decade of that stepper, i.e., is put in series with decade 2.

Decade switches associated with the 1st stages of the steppers.

Decade switches associated with the 2nd stages of the steppers.

Decade switches associated with the 3rd stages of the steppers.

Decade switches associated with the 4th stages of the steppers.

Decade switches associated with the 5th stages of the steppers.

Decade switches associated with the 6th stages of the steppers.

Stepper clear switch

This switch determines the number of stages of the stepper and associated decade switches which are used. After the stepper gets to the stage set on its clear switch and counts to the number set on the corresponding decade switches it clears to its first position instead of stepping to the next position.

Terminals Adi,.....,Kdi - Stepper direct input terminals.

Pulses supplied to one of these terminals will be counted by the stepper. These pulses may be either program pulses or digit pulses. If digit pulses are used the stepper clear switch must be set to 6.

The stepper will count modulo c, where c is the setting of the stepper clear switch.

A program pulse is emitted from one of the stepper program pulse output terminals one addition time after a program pulse is received on the stepper program pulse input terminal . This pulse is emitted from the terminal corresponding to the state of the stepper at the time it is emitted. The stepper may be stepped or cleared at the same time without effecting that pulse.

No pulse should be supplied to this terminal at the same time as a stepping action is caused by the decades.

tively with decades 1, 2,....,20.

e pulses may be either program or digit
ade switches corresponding to position
must be a program pulse.
its decade of a stepper one addition
nal of that stepper.
the units decade only at times when there

MOORE SCHOOL OF ELECTRICAL ENGINEERING			
UNIVERSITY OF PENNSYLVANIA			
MASTER PROGRAMMER FRONT PANEL NO. 2			
MATERIAL	FINISH		SCALE
Drawn by: J. EDELSACK DEC. 1944	Checked by:	Approved by:	PX-8-302

1

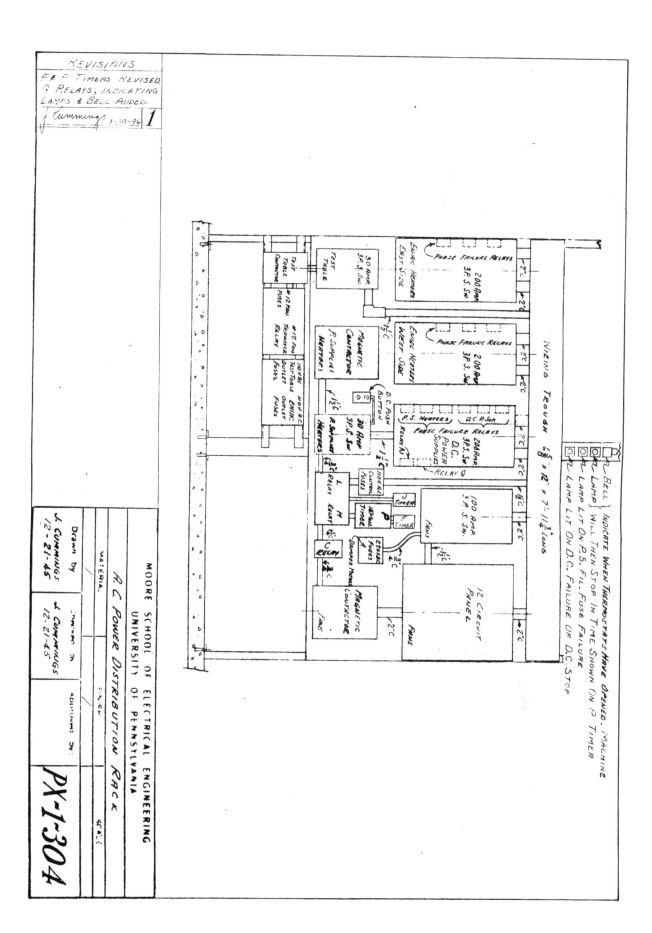

REVISIONS

F. & P. TIMERS REVISED.
Q RELAYS, INDICATING
LAMPS & BELL ADDED.

J. Cummings 1-30-96 | 1

MOORE SCHOOL OF ELECTRICAL ENGINEERING
UNIVERSITY OF PENNSYLVANIA

A.C. POWER DISTRIBUTION RACK

Drawn by
J. Cummings
12-21-45

J. Cummings
12-21-45

MATERIAL.   FINISH.   ADDITIONS ON:

PX-1-304

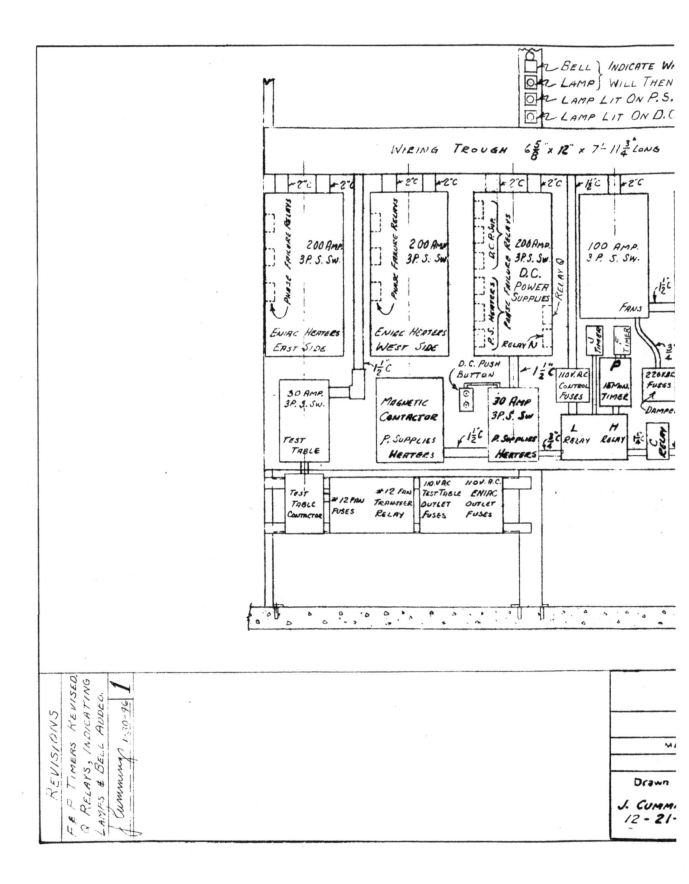

BELL ⎫ INDICATE W...
LAMP ⎬ WILL THEN...
LAMP LIT ON P.S.
LAMP LIT ON D.C...

WIRING TROUGH 6⅝" × 12" × 7'-11¾" LONG

2"C   2"C   2"C   2"C   2"C   2"C   1½"C   2"C

200 AMP.
3 P. S. SW.

PHASE FAILURE RELAYS

ENIAC HEATERS
EAST SIDE

200 AMP.
3 P. S. SW.

PHASE FAILURE RELAYS

ENIAC HEATERS
WEST SIDE

200 AMP.
3 P. S. SW.
D.C.
POWER
SUPPLIES

D.C. P. SUP.
P.S. HEATERS
PHASE FAILURE RELAYS
RELAY Q
RELAY N

100 AMP.
3 P. S. SW.

FANS

1½"C

30 AMP.
3 P. S. SW.

TEST
TABLE

1½"C

MAGNETIC
CONTACTOR

P. SUPPLIES
HEATERS

D.C. PUSH
BUTTON

1½"C

30 AMP.
3 P.S. SW

P. SUPPLIES
HEATERS

1½"C

110 V. A.C.
CONTROL
FUSES

J TIMER
F TIMER

15 MIN.
TIMER

P

L
RELAY

H
RELAY

220 V.A.C.
FUSES

DAMPER

C
RELAY

TEST
TABLE
CONTACTOR

#12 FAN
FUSES

#12 FAN
TRANSFER
RELAY

110 V.A.C.
TEST TABLE
OUTLET
FUSES

110 V. A.C.
ENIAC
OUTLET
FUSES

REVISIONS
F & P TIMERS REVISED.
Q RELAYS, INDICATING
LAMPS & BELL ADDED.
J. Cummings 1-30-96   1

M...

Drawn

J. CUMM...
12-21-...

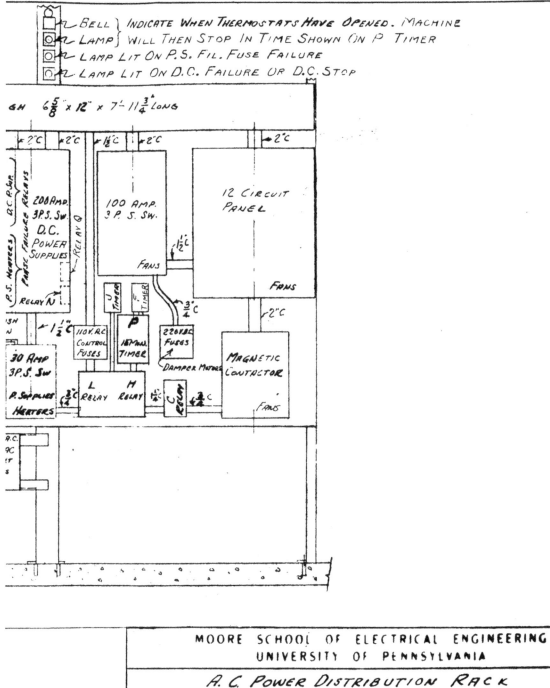

- Bell } INDICATE WHEN THERMOSTATS HAVE OPENED. MACHINE
- Lamp } WILL THEN STOP IN TIME SHOWN ON P TIMER
- Lamp LIT ON P.S. FIL. FUSE FAILURE
- Lamp LIT ON D.C. FAILURE OR D.C. STOP

GH $6\frac{5}{8}$" × 12" × 7'-11$\frac{3}{4}$" LONG

←2"C   ←2"C   ←1$\frac{1}{2}$C   ←2"C   ←2"C

200 Amp. 3 P.S. Sw.

D.C. POWER SUPPLIES

RELAY Q

P.S. Heaters | Fuse Failure Relays | D.C.P. Gen

RELAY N

100 Amp. 3 P. S. Sw.

FANS

1$\frac{1}{2}$C

12 CIRCUIT PANEL

FANS

2"C

←1$\frac{1}{2}$C

ISH N

J Timer

$\frac{3}{4}$C

30 Amp 3 P.S. Sw

P. Supplies
HEATERS

110V. A.C. CONTROL FUSES

P
18 Min. TIMER

220 V.A.C. FUSES
DAMPER MOTORS

$\frac{3}{4}$C | L RELAY | M RELAY | 1$\frac{1}{4}$C | C RELAY | $\frac{3}{4}$C

MAGNETIC CONTACTOR

FANS

A.C.
PC
IT
S

MOORE SCHOOL OF ELECTRICAL ENGINEERING
UNIVERSITY OF PENNSYLVANIA

A. C. POWER DISTRIBUTION RACK

MATERIAL	FINISH	SCALE	
/	/		
Drawn by	Checked by	APPROVED BY:	PX-1-304
J. CUMMINGS 12-21-45	J. CUMMINGS 12-21-45		

The mechnical torpedo data computer provided firing solutions for U.S. Navy submariners during the first half of WWII. This Mark 3 manual provides a fascinating glimpse inside this mechanical wonder.

Designed by Swedish cryptographer Boris Hagelin, the M-209 Converter was a portable mechanical cipher machine. This M-209 Technical Manual describes the operation and care of this fascinating device and provides a fascinating glimpse into mid-level encryption technology circa 1944.

Also now available!
www.PeriscopeFilm.com